NARROWING THE LITERACY GAP

SOLVING PROBLEMS IN THE TEACHING OF LITERACY

Cathy Collins Block, *Series Editor*

RECENT VOLUMES

Rethinking Reading Comprehension
Edited by Anne P. Sweet and Catherine E. Snow

Exemplary Literacy Teachers: Promoting Success for All Children in Grades K–5
Cathy Collins Block and John N. Mangieri

Assessment for Reading Instruction
Michael C. McKenna and Steven A. Stahl

Vocabulary Instruction: Research to Practice
Edited by James F. Baumann and Edward J. Kame'enui

The Reading Specialist: Leadership for the Classroom, School, and Community
Rita M. Bean

Multicultural and Multilingual Literacy and Language: Contexts and Practices
Edited by Fenice B. Boyd and Cynthia H. Brock, with Mary S. Rozendal

Teaching All the Children: Strategies for Developing Literacy in an Urban Setting
Edited by Diane Lapp, Cathy Collins Block, Eric J. Cooper,
James Flood, Nancy Roser, and Josefina Villamil Tinajero

Conceptual Foundations of Teaching Reading
Mark Sadoski

The Literacy Coach's Handbook: A Guide to Research-Based Practice
Sharon Walpole and Michael C. McKenna

Comprehension Process Instruction: Creating Reading Success in Grades K–3
Cathy Collins Block, Lori L. Rodgers, and Rebecca B. Johnson

Adolescent Literacy Research and Practice
Edited by Tamara L. Jetton and Janice A. Dole

Tutoring Adolescent Literacy Learners: A Guide for Volunteers
Kelly Chandler-Olcott and Kathleen A. Hinchman

Success with Struggling Readers: The Benchmark School Approach
Irene West Gaskins

Making Sense of Phonics: The Hows and Whys
Isabel L. Beck

Reading Instruction That Works, Third Edition: The Case for Balanced Teaching
Michael Pressley

Narrowing the Literacy Gap: What Works in High-Poverty Schools
Diane M. Barone

Narrowing the Literacy Gap

What Works in High-Poverty Schools

DIANE M. BARONE

THE GUILFORD PRESS
New York   London

©2006 The Guilford Press
A Division of Guilford Publications, Inc.
72 Spring Street, New York, NY 10012
www.guilford.com

Printed in the United States of America

This book is printed on acid-free paper.

Last digit is print number: 9 8 7 6 5 4 3 2 1

Library of Congress Cataloging-in-Publication Data

Barone, Diane M.
 Narrowing the literacy gap : what works in high-poverty schools /
Diane M. Barone.
    p. cm. — (Solving problems in the teaching of literacy)
 Includes bibliographical references and index.
 ISBN-10 1-59385-277-0 ISBN-13 978-1-59385-277-1 (hardcover : alk. paper) —
 ISBN-10 1-59385-276-2   ISBN-13 978-1-59385-276-4 (pbk. : alk. paper)
  1. Reading (Elementary)—United States—Case studies.   2. Remedial
reading—United States.   3. Poor children—Education—United States.
4. Urban schools—United States.   I. Title. II. Series.
 LB1573.B3587 2006
                                                       2005033255

About the Author

Diane M. Barone, EdD, is Professor in the Department of Educational Specialties at the University of Nevada, Reno, where she teaches courses in literacy and qualitative research methods. Her research has focused primarily on young children's literacy development, particularly in high-poverty schools. She has conducted two longitudinal studies of literacy development: a 4-year study of children exposed prenatally to crack/cocaine, and a 7-year study of children in a high-poverty school. Her publications include articles in the *Journal of Literacy Research, Elementary School Journal, The Reading Teacher, Gifted Childhood Quarterly,* and *Research in the Teaching of English*; book chapters in *Educational Resiliency, Literacy and Young Children,* and *Literacy Research Methods*; and a number of books, including *Developing Literacy,* with Donald Bear; *Resilient Children; The National Board Handbook,* with National Board Teachers; *Teaching Early Literacy: Development, Assessment, and Instruction,* with Marla Mallette and Shelley Xu; *Research-Based Practices in Early Literacy,* with Lesley Morrow; *Reading First in the Classroom,* with Darrin Hardman and Joan Taylor; and *Improving Student Writing, K–8,* with Joan Taylor. Dr. Barone served for 8 years as the Editor of *Reading Research Quarterly,* and is currently a board member of the National Reading Conference and the International Reading Association, as well as the principal investigator of the Reading First grant in Nevada.

Preface

The book *Narrowing the Literacy Gap: What Works in High-Poverty Schools* is centered in a 7-year, longitudinal study. This study was guided by a simple question: Why did students in high-poverty schools struggle with literacy achievement? I wondered why there were such negative reports about the literacy learning of students in high-poverty schools. For example, Goldenberg (2001) wrote:

> A low-SES child attending a low-income school and living in a low-income community is at far greater risk for reading difficulties than is the same child attending and living in a middle- or high-income school and community. (p. 217)

The evidence was clear: Students in high-poverty schools struggled with literacy, as documented by standardized achievement tests. But why?

I decided that the only way to answer this question was to design a research study in which I observed the literacy learning and instruction of a group of students in a high-poverty school from their first days in kindergarten to their last day in sixth grade. This study focused on the in-school literacy experiences of students. This design structure was put in place because children in high-poverty schools are more dependent on their school experiences for literacy development than are students in middle-class schools (Alexander & Entwisle, 1996).

The results of this lengthy study are shared in this book. Chapter 1 explores why it is important to study children's literacy learning and instruction over time. Readers learn about the school chosen for the study and the literacy instruction provided to students. In Chapter 2, a close look at student learning is shared. Readers become familiar with the development of all of the focal students by following their journey through elementary school.

In Chapter 3, the lens shifts its focus from students to teachers. Teachers move to the foreground and students to the background, so that teachers' planned and unplanned enactments related to literacy instruction are examined. I believe it is not possible to understand the learning demonstrated by students without investigating the instruction they have received. In Chapter 4, which departs from the descriptions of teaching and learning shared in Chapters 1, 2, and 3, I move to a more complex view of learning and teaching. I try on different theoretical lenses, so that the more complex, messier view of literacy is explored. The data were reanalyzed through a social-constructivist perspective, positioning theory, and resilience theory. Each lens provides additional information in describing literacy learning, and when considered together, they allow readers to examine the complex dynamic surrounding literacy learning.

In the final chapter, interesting conundrums, such as balancing high-stakes testing with teaching, are discussed. Two exemplary teachers are showcased to validate the importance of teachers to student learning. The chapter concludes with several major discoveries of this study, followed by an Appendix for those readers interested in the details of the research study's methods.

This book is distinctive in that it offers one of the few opportunities to view student learning and teaching over time. It documents the connection between student learning and teaching. It provides rich descriptions of the day-to-day learning experiences of students in a high-poverty school. It suggests ways that teachers and principals in high-poverty schools can support and enhance literacy learning, so that all students are successful. Moreover, it highlights the complexity of teaching and learning through multilayered interpretations and descriptions of students and teachers.

REFERENCES

Alexander, K., & Entwisle, D. (1996). Schools and children at risk. In A. Booth & J. Dunn (Eds.), *Family and school links: How do they affect educational outcomes?* (pp. 67–88). Mahwah, NJ: Erlbaum.

Goldenberg, C. (2001). Making schools work for low-income families in the 21st century. In S. B. Neuman & D. K. Dickinson (Eds.), *Handbook of early literacy research* (Vol. 1, pp. 211–231). New York: Guilford Press.

Contents

Chapter 1   Learning from Students over Time   1

Chapter 2   Looking at Students' Literacy Learning   25

Chapter 3   Learning from Teachers   79

Chapter 4   Widening the Lens: Multiple Perspectives   115
on Teaching and Learning

Chapter 5   Conundrums and Discoveries Along   151
the Way

Appendix   Methodology of the Research Study   181

Index   189

Learning from Students over Time

The day after Labor Day, mother walked me the six
blocks to the two-story red brick Fernwood Grammar
School, where I joined a confusion of children from the
first through the eighth grades. Mother left me with other
first graders in the basement. . . . Clutching our books,
tablets, and pencil boxes, we were all excited and
bewildered. (pp. 74–75)

By the end of second grade I could read, although outside
of school I flatly refused to open a book. (p. 89)

The teacher put her hand on my shoulder, turned, and
smiled at the other teacher. "This one," she said, "is a
nuisance." (p. 100)

Miss Smith had standards. We could read, but we must
read good books. Cheap series books, traded around the
neighborhood, were not permitted in her classroom. Miss
Smith was strict. She once made me stay after school
until I could write on the blackboard, from memory and
in order, all the presidents of the United States. I do not
recall what I did to deserve this judgment, but I do recall
thinking it more sensible than writing "I will not talk in
the gymnasium" one hundred times. (p. 144)

These quotes come from Beverly Cleary's memoir *A Girl
from Yamhill* (1988), where she highlights her experiences in elementary and high school. As shared here, some of these experiences were
positive and others, particularly when she was called a "nuisance" or

made to write the names of the presidents, were not. Collected together, there is a picture of Cleary's schooling and her learning that
vacillates between success and frustration. Her memories provide a
vivid picture of her school experiences from year to year.

In a similar way, this book is centered on the literacy experiences
of children as they were enrolled in a high-poverty elementary
school. Like Cleary's book, a view is shared of students' literacy
learning and instruction as they moved through elementary school,
grade by grade. Unlike Cleary's work, this book is centered in a longitudinal study with the explicit focus of learning about literacy
learning and instruction, not just in memoirs written by the students
or their teachers at the end of their elementary school experiences.

THE IMPORTANCE OF STUDYING
CHILDREN OVER TIME

In 1986, Stanovich documented the importance of learning to read in
the early grades and how success in learning to read affects later
school achievement. Juel's work (1988, 1994) concluded that a child
who was a poor reader in the first grade would most likely be a poor
reader in the fourth grade, and it would be difficult for this child ever
to attain grade-level achievement. Both of these researchers highlighted the importance of phonological awareness in building reading
success. Students who did not develop this ability to manipulate
sounds in the primary grades were struggling readers in later grades.
They also noted that students from high-poverty backgrounds tended
to have poor phonological awareness, and thus more difficulty learning to read and write.

Moreover, Stanovich (1986, 1993) discussed the consequences
of early reading difficulty. He reasoned that since poor readers
avoided reading and were often assigned texts at a frustration level,
they did not gain understanding of text, vocabulary, and other benefits of being actively engaged with reading. Therefore, struggling
readers read less often and had reduced exposure to text. This lack of
exposure contributed to the continuing gap between good and poor
readers. Stanovich called this the *Matthew effect,* in which students

who read more got richer or knew more about the world and how to interact with text. Students who did not read got poorer, because they did not have the knowledge or vocabulary of their peers—critical knowledge for understanding text with more abstract concepts.

The research of Anderson, Wilson, and Fielding (1988) complemented Stanovich's work by showing a positive relationship between the measure of amount of reading and measures such as reading comprehension, reading fluency, and vocabulary. Results from this study indicated that fifth-grade students who read the most scored in the 98th percentile on achievement tests and read about 65 minutes a day. Fifth-grade students who read books for less than a minute each day scored in the 10th percentile on achievement tests.

Although these studies are important in demonstrating how students who get behind stay behind, they do not illuminate the experiences of students on a day-to-day basis. They also do not specifically focus on high-poverty students, students who often are noted for their less than successful achievement in school, or students coming to school with a home language other than English (Allington & Walmsley, 1995; Moll & Diaz, 1987; Snow, Burns, & Griffin, 1998).

I wondered why children, especially children in high-poverty schools, were not more successful in literacy achievement (Dyson, 2001). While the gloomy statistics are common knowledge among teachers and policymakers, the day-to-day practices encountered by such students are not. Neufeld and Fitzgerald (2001) state, "The need is great to describe and understand what happens in regard to these young at-risk readers" (p. 98). This is especially true since so many of these students are learning to speak English as they are learning to read and write in English, and there are few descriptions of this process (Garcia, 2000). Tabors and Snow (2001) report that there is little research on early literacy acquisition of bilingual children, and there is a compelling practical urgency to understand this process, because so many students who are learning English as a new language (ELLs) have lower achievement scores than their monolingual peers.

In response to these needs, I designed a study that focused on the day-to-day learning of students in a high-poverty school. Studying the literacy learning of students over time is no simple task for many reasons. From a simple viewpoint, one might ask: What is the developmental course of children's literacy acquisition in a high-poverty school? Certainly, this question can be answered through systematic observation over time, but is this sufficient? Just knowing about children's literacy development does not get at how teachers support or hinder it. So this myopic view of children's development needs to be amalgamated into teachers' organization, instructional practices, and expectations. In doing so, the relationships between student development and the instruction provided can be explored. However, this view is still linear, in that student development and instruction are explored in a systematic, grade-by-grade method. Is this linear view enough? I do not believe so, for it ignores the social constructions of literacy, or the messy, nonlinear view. As Dyson (2001) writes:

> Learning about written language is not just about learning a new code for representing meanings. It is about entering new social dialogues in an expanding life world. As such, written language learning is inevitably a part of learning about social and ideological worlds and about the place of a child's own relationships and experiences in those worlds. (p. 138)

Within this book, both linear and nonlinear explorations are pursued to provide a multifaceted understanding of student literacy development. In addition to learning about literacy growth and instruction, I have embraced the complexity and messiness of student learning in social situations. These more complex views incorporate learning about student identity and the positioning or power relationships shared by teachers, students, and peers. These varied paths of inquiry were necessary, because student learning and teaching are intricate and intertwined. As a researcher, I recorded the social and academic dynamic of the classroom, where, on some occasions, the focal students were in the foreground, and at other times they receded, with a teacher moving to the foreground (Dyson & Genishi, 2005). Away from the study site, I recursively studied these notes to reveal multiple interpretations of learning in a high-poverty school. Importantly, each path's results contribute to a synergistic understanding of literacy learning and instruction over 7 years.

EXEMPLARY LITERACY LEARNING
AND INSTRUCTION

Before I began a 7-year exploration of students' literacy learning and instruction, I synthesized the research related to these areas to guide my work. This synthesis included literacy learning that moved from early literacy development to the more sophisticated reading and writing abilities of intermediate grade students. And parallel to this synthesis was an exploration of the exemplary teaching practices that often subtly varied from grade level to grade level.

My syntheses focused on in-school literacy learning and instruction, and seemed to ignore home literacy practices. This focus was not meant to negate the important literacy experiences in which children engaged in their home environments. Rather, it was based on the knowledge that low-income children rely more on the school and school literacy practices for their academic development than do middle-class children (Alexander & Entwisle, 1996). Therefore, my focus in this study was on the school and not on home literacy practices.

Primary Grades

Reading and writing achievement in the primary grades provide the critical foundation for a child's future academic success. Early reading and writing achievement increase the likelihood that children will continue to read, thus acquiring knowledge in a multitude of content-related domains such as science or social studies (Cunningham & Stanovich, 1998). Coupled with this knowledge comes increased vocabulary, and the ability to read and understand complex text, particularly informational text (Allington, 1984).

Although all grade levels are important to literacy learning, first grade is often singled out as a benchmark year for literacy development. Snow et al. (1998) observed that quality instruction provided during this year was the best intervention to prevent later reading difficulty. Hiebert, Pearson, Taylor, Richardson, and Paris (1997) discovered that children as young as first graders identified themselves as good or poor readers, and that these identities colored further reading achievement.

Researchers have documented the specific early literacy knowledge that is important to later achievement. There is consistent agreement that phonological awareness is critical for young children's reading development (National Reading Panel, 2000; Snow et al., 1998; Yopp & Yopp, 2000). Children need to manipulate the phonemes in words through sound matching or rhyming for instance. Additionally, Adams (1990) identified the importance of letter knowledge to future success. Torgeson and Davis (1996) noted that kindergartners' ability to engage in invented spelling, which demonstrates phonological knowledge, is a strong predictor of future achievement. Vocabulary size and the understanding of spoken language have similarly been identified as predictors of future achievement (Hart & Risley, 1999; Share, Jorm, MacLean, & Mathews, 1984).

Pressley (1998) and Snow et al. (1998) suggested the following broad areas that are critical to young students' future literacy achievement:

1. *Understanding and using the alphabetic principle.* Students have phonological awareness, letter–sound knowledge, and efficient decoding abilities. The combination of these results in comprehension of text.
2. *Understanding of print functions.* Students know the purposes for reading and writing and can express themselves in writing.
3. *Vocabulary and knowledge.* Students have sufficient knowledge and vocabulary to understand the material they read.
4. *Motivation to engage in reading and writing.* Students frequently read and write to communicate and enjoy these experiences.

By the end of the primary grades, students are expected to have full understanding of sound–symbol relationships in single-syllable words, fluency in reading, and the ability to comprehend narrative and informational text.

Intermediate Grades

The expectations for reading and writing become more complex and harder to discern as students move into the intermediate grades—

grades 4 through 6. Allington and Johnston (2002) write, "Fourth grade has been the point where informational texts became central to the curriculum and where students were expected to begin to acquire information from those texts" (p. 16). This is a huge shift for students as they now move from narrative text to informational text as their primary instructional tool. They must learn about the organizational structures of informational text, such as description or cause and effect, and increased vocabulary demands. There are also dramatic changes in the narrative texts they explore. They shift from books with much illustrative support to novels that require attention to details of plot and characters over several days or weeks of reading. They are also asked to write reports or longer narrative pieces that are not completed in a single attempt.

Learning to read is very visible; for example, a child represents a *b* for *bug* and can soon write the word and read a simple informational text about bugs. Learning to read in the intermediate grades is more opaque. For example, students are expected to

1. *Become more fluent in their reading.* Students in third grade are expected to read about 130 words per minute at the end of the year, whereas sixth graders are expected to read about 200 words per minute at the end of the year (Rasinski, 2004). Slow readers have more difficulty comprehending text and find completing assigned reading difficult to impossible.

2. *Comprehend deeply.* Students move from a more central focus on literal comprehension of narrative text to inferential understanding of both narrative and informational text (Raphael, 2000). This understanding includes critical analysis across texts, as well as within a text.

3. *Engage in sustained reading and writing.* Students are reading and writing longer texts. Their focus extends over days and weeks rather than a single day or episode (Raphael, 2000).

4. *Develop larger vocabulary.* Students are expected to know both concrete and abstract word vocabulary. By the end of eighth grade, the expected student vocabulary includes 25,000 words (Graves, 2000). This expectation tends to be more difficult to achieve for ELLs.

5. *Understand the representations of multisyllabic words.* Stu-

dents acquire the ability to add prefixes and suffixes to words. They learn about the meanings of roots and can generalize them across words. For example, they know that *mal* means evil (Bear, Invernizzi, Templeton, & Johnston, 2004).

These are important milestones for students; however, they are less visible to students, teachers, and parents than simply learning to read. For this reason, parents and teachers are often unaware of the challenges in acquiring this more sophisticated knowledge and understanding about literacy. For example, students require careful instruction to help them understand the structures of informational text so that they can comprehend it and recognize the careful reading this kind of text requires.

EXEMPLARY LITERACY INSTRUCTION FOR STUDENTS FROM HIGH-POVERTY BACKGROUNDS AND ELLs

Once children enter school, classrooms become the most important context to support academic achievement, particularly for students from high-poverty backgrounds. Classroom climate, particularly the relationship between the teacher and students, is critical to students' success (Dillon, 2000). Nieto (1999) recommends that teachers build positive relationships with students and their parents, as a way for students to succeed in school. Delpit (1995) and Ladson-Billings (1994) encourage teachers to have high expectations for students and to value each student's academic progress. Nieto (1999) and Ladson-Billings (1994) view a nurturing environment in the classroom to be as critical to student achievement as an appropriate literacy curriculum that meets the needs of individual students. Furthermore, McDermott's (1977) classic study reinforces the importance of having trusting relationships between a teacher and students, because these relationships are the most essential ingredient to student success, more important than a teaching approach or strategy.

As specific recommendations are identified for exemplary literacy instruction in the following sections, they are grounded in the belief that the teacher is the most important element to student achievement. In high-poverty schools, such teachers do not wallow in the demographics associated with their students; rather, they identify and extend the personal and academic potential within each student. Students achieve the highest literacy expectations when they are in a classroom with a caring teacher who has high expectations and uses exemplary literacy practices. The synergy between a teacher and exemplary strategies is what makes a difference in student learning.

Primary Grades

Literacy instruction for young children has recently been guided by the National Reading Panel report (2000). This report highlights the need to be systematic about the instruction in phonological awareness, phonics, comprehension, fluency, and vocabulary presented to students. All of these areas are important to the development of young readers and writers. Importantly, phonological awareness and phonics are more prevalent in preschool through first grade and diminish in focus as students enter second or third grade.

Pressley, Rankin, and Yokoi (1996) studied the teaching practices of exemplary first-grade teachers. They learned that these teachers created classrooms filled with print and included writing materials, a class library, and numerous other books for students to read and explore. Children in these classrooms heard a multitude of stories and informational text daily. When teachers read to students, they often stopped to let students know what they were thinking, to focus on an interesting word, or to allow students to share comments related to reading.

Beyond these elements, teachers modeled comprehension and writing strategies, used multiple grouping arrangements, and were sensitive to individual student strengths and needs. These teachers balanced their literacy instruction by focusing on meaning-making activities and strategies, along with word-level and decoding activities. When students read, the teacher encouraged prediction and used choral and shared reading to support novice readers. Students' writing included stories, responses to literature, and informational writing. These teachers were masters at formally and informally assessing students and using this information to guide instruction. Summing up, these researchers credit student achievement to teachers' use of high-quality literature, attention to sound–symbol relationships, writing, and infrequent use of round-robin reading, along with efforts to meet the individual needs of their students.

Block and Mangieri (2003) expanded on the work of Pressley et al. (1996) by carefully studying the unique qualities of exemplary teachers from kindergarten though fifth grade. Teachers at each grade level had distinctive strengths that contributed to student learning. The following strengths are noted for primary grade teachers:

- *Kindergarten teachers*—"Guardians is the role that exemplary kindergarten teachers most often assume. They are Guardians of children's discoveries about print, and they cherish students' first attempts to read, however feeble these may be. Guardians are highly skilled at using daily observations rather than printed texts to guide their instruction" (p. 40).
- *First-grade teachers*—"Encouragers and supporters are the two dominant roles performed most frequently by exemplary first-grade teachers" (p. 41). These teachers are described by the complexity of teaching that they orchestrate. They are able to teach multiple skills based on student need and know how to develop students' literacy understandings. Moreover, they are excellent record keepers, who can match informal assessments to student instruction.
- *Second-grade teachers*—"Demonstrators is the dominant role of exemplary second-grade teachers" (p. 43). These teachers engage students in important conversations around texts. Second-grade teachers offer students other approaches for learning phonics, decoding, or comprehension. Second-grade teachers are "able to formulate an effective and novel approach to demonstrate a confusing literacy concept on the spot, when students become confused or frustrated while reading" (p. 43).
- *Third-grade teachers*—"Managers is the dominant role assumed by exemplary literacy teachers of third-grade students. Managers demonstrate exceptional talent in working with varied groups and multilevel materials simultaneously. These teachers show exceptional expertise in making transitions and in bridging the gap from learning to read to reading to learn. . . . They ground their instruction in providing ways that their students can gather information from text" (p. 44).

A complementary study by Taylor, Pearson, Clark, and Walpole (1999) investigated accomplished teachers in first through third grades in schools with low-income students. They found that time spent in small-group instruction differentiated the most effective teachers. In small groups, teachers explicitly taught how to comprehend narrative and expository text, phonics instruction, vocabulary instruction, and so on. Often, effective teachers used resource teachers during small-group instruction, so that the majority of students worked with a professional during this time. These teachers also used informal assessment to guide instruction and the composition of students within each grouping.

Taylor et al. (1999) also discovered that effective teachers provided time for independent reading for about one-half hour each day. These teachers not only taught phonics but also supported students in using their phonics knowledge to identify words in text. Finally, the researchers discovered that exemplary teachers spent more time each day teaching reading, approximately 134 minutes, than less accomplished teachers.

To summarize the research on instruction in the primary grades, teachers in each grade level contribute in a special way to the development of each student's literacy knowledge and understanding. Students begin with instruction targeted to print and its structure (e.g., left to right, top to bottom), the alphabet and its sound–symbol relationships, vocabulary, and meaning gained from text (McGee & Richgels, 2003). Subsequent teachers build on these beginning concepts so that by the closure of third grade, students can express themselves in writing, comprehend and understand narrative and informational text, are fluent with reading, and have expanded vocabularies. Importantly, primary grade teachers focus on reading throughout their day and provide numerous opportunities for direct instruction, guided practice, and independent practice.

Intermediate Grades

As with primary grade teachers, Allington and Johnston (2002) acknowledge that the teacher and his or her relationships with students are more important than the instructional program that is used. While there is less research on intermediate teachers, Snow, Barnes, Chandler, Goodman, and Hemphill (1991) observed second- and fourth-grade teachers to learn about the instructional characteristics of the most successful teachers. The numerous characteristics they found include the following:

- Explicit instruction
- Behavioral routines
- Involving students in challenging curriculum
- Creating classroom climates that are welcoming to students
- Many student–teacher academic conversations
- Providing a wealth of reading materials
- Ongoing and frequent library visits
- Challenging curricular activities that engage students
- Reliance on inferential questions
- Displaying student work

They discovered that students placed for numerous years in classrooms with teachers who had these characteristics had higher student achievement. This proved true even in schools where teachers were using the same core programs for instruction.

Knapp (1995) studied classrooms in high-poverty elementary schools across three states. He learned that students had higher reading achievement in meaning-centered classrooms than in skills-based classrooms. In these meaning-oriented classrooms, students had many opportunities to read; used reading and writing in other subjects, such as science and social studies; always were concerned with achieving meaning; and had numerous opportunities to chat about reading and writing. Similar to Snow et al. (1991), Knapp (1995) discovered that the choice of core program did not affect the differences noted between highly skilled and less-skilled teachers.

In addition to studying first-grade exemplary teachers, Pressley, Wharton-McDonald, Mistretta-Hampston, and Echevarria (1998) studied exemplary fourth- and fifth-grade teachers. They discovered a great variability among these teachers' instructional methods and the way they used materials. They learned that these teachers implemented the following:

1. A multitude of grouping patterns—whole group, small group, conferencing one-to-one
2. Inferential, critical, and literal questions
3. Vocabulary development as a main focus of instruction
4. A variety of curriculum materials
5. Reading and writing in the content areas

Finally, although Block and Mangieri (2003) did not study exemplary teacher characteristics in sixth-grade teachers, they did explore fourth- and fifth-grade teachers. They learned the following:

• *Fourth-grade teachers*—"Coaches is the dominant role and manner in which exemplary fourth-grade teachers carry out their literacy responsibilities" (p. 45). Fourth-grade teachers motivate students in many different ways. They are effective in helping students extract information from text. They facilitate comprehension of science and social studies texts that moves from literal to inferential and critical comprehension.

• *Fifth-grade teachers*—"Adaptors is the dominant responsibility that exemplary fifth-grade teachers normally embrace. They demonstrate special competence in being able to divide up and teach large amounts of knowledge in learnable chunks so that their students will want to learn" (p. 48). Fifth-grade teachers work on student self-esteem as they facilitate the learning of extensive content knowledge.

Intermediate teachers extend the literacy foundation developed by primary grade teachers, so that students can readily understand both fictional and informational text. They use varied approaches and materials to facilitate literacy development. Therefore, no single description fits each and every exemplary teacher in the intermediate grades. However, they consistently expand on the literacy knowledge and skills that students have acquired in the primary grades by targeting instruction to individual students' strengths and needs.

Students Learning English as a New Language

The previous descriptions of student learning and instruction are pertinent for ELLs; however, additional issues need to be considered. As classrooms and schools have more students coming to them who have a primary language other than English, the need to accelerate these students' literacy achievement is pressing. Reglin (1995) documented that, unfortunately, teachers often have lower expectations for these students. As a result of these lower expectations, they often require less of such students, which results in an emphasis on basic facts; low-level, single-answer questions; fewer challenging assignments; and so on. Contrary to these practices, Nieto (1999) discussed the need for schools and teachers to engage in demanding curricula, to respect a child's home language and culture, to have high expectations for students, and to involve parents so that students are successful. Similar to the work of Knapp (1995), Moll and Diaz (1987) considered classrooms where Hispanic students developed into successful or not very successful readers and writers. They discovered that teachers who highlighted text meaning and comprehension produced students who had high achievement in reading.

Gutierrez, Basquedano-Lopez, and Turner (1997) recounted the importance of language when they wrote that "language is a tool we use to express and make sense of our experience; it is a tool that transforms our thinking" (p. 369). The centrality of language to learning is an issue that teachers wrestle with as they provide exemplary instruction to learners who are learning English as they read and write in English. School experiences for English-speaking students are based in their home language and support an easier transition from home to school. The teacher's major responsibility with these students is to facilitate movement from home language, typically more informal, to the academic language used in schools (Beykont, 2002; Tabors & Snow, 2001). There are additional challenges when teachers work with ELLs, because they must help students move from home to school language, and they must support students in learning English as a language for conversation and learning (Cummins, 2003). Gutierrez et al. (1997) remind us that this is a huge undertaking for students and teachers alike, for students' conceptions of language, literacy, and culturally appropriate ways of doing school "are influenced by the experiences they bring to school, their previous instructional settings, and the ongoing activities that teachers and students construct in classrooms" (p. 369). When students enter classrooms where English is the only language of instruction, the rich language and experiential backgrounds of ELLs are dismissed and sometimes denied value in schools. Gutierrez (2001) states, "Language, the most powerful mediating tool for mediating learning, in this case the children's primary language, is excluded from the students' learning tool kit" (p. 565).

A common situation for many ELLs is that upon entry into school, typically kindergarten, they are expected to communicate only through a new language, English. In most schools, these students are expected to achieve the same literacy competencies as their peers who come to school with a home language of English. Very few of these students ever have extra time in school to learn about reading and writing in English while they learn English. They are typically allotted the same amount of time to meet grade-level expectations as students who come to school familiar with English. This is an enormous challenge for students, teachers, and parents (Nieto, 1999).

Cummins (2003) provided suggestions for what teachers can do to build English competency as students learn to read and write concurrently in English. He suggested that teachers facilitate conversational fluency with students. For most students, this can take 1 or 2 years to develop. Although academic language takes longer to develop, up to 8 years, teachers simultaneously develop discrete language skills and academic language proficiency that includes the vocabulary only experienced in textbooks as children are becoming facile with informal English.

Fillmore (1997) identified the following explicit activities and strategies that teachers can use to facilitate ELLs' literacy learning:

- Help students make sense of text.
- Call attention to the way language is used in text.
- Discuss the meaning and interpretation of phrases and sentences.
- Make connections across texts to common vocabulary.

- Help students discover grammatical cues that signal relationships like cause and effect. (p. 4)

Instruction for ELLs often overlaps with the recommended instruction for all students. In all of the information about exemplary teachers, a central discovery is that they provide language-rich classrooms where children explore the details of print, while also focusing on the meaning gained from text. Unique to the instruction recommended for ELLs is the focus on language and the support students need as they simultaneously learn English and learn to read and write in this new language. Importantly, Gutierrez (2001) notes that ELLs must build a new language tool kit to accomplish literacy proficiency in English-only classrooms. This new tool kit takes time to develop as children adjust the knowledge they have in their home language to the new language and behavioral expectations of school.

AN OVERVIEW OF THE STUDY

The School

From this theoretical background centered on literacy instruction and learning, I began a 7-year study of 16 children in a high-poverty elementary school. This study began with the selection of a high-poverty school. I chose Howard Elementary, for it is one of the oldest schools in a midsize urban school district. The neighborhood surrounding the school is eclectic in that there are homes, apartments, and public housing. There are also several churches near the school, and a regional library and a middle school border the school property. Howard has a long history of poor achievement scores, although, in the last few years, it has met annual yearly progress mandates. This past year, 80% of Howard's fourth-grade students scored in the two lowest quartiles in reading on the Iowa Test of Basic Skills (ITBS), and on the state writing assessment, 60% of fourth grades were approaching the standards.

Howard teachers are very aware of the low scores their students achieve on assessment measures. During the time I was studying in their school, they participated in the following endeavors to raise student achievement:

1. A balanced literacy program throughout the school. Teachers received ongoing professional development in literacy to help them implement exemplary literacy practices, such as shared or guided reading.
2. Blocked literacy instructional time—all morning in the primary grades and all afternoon in the intermediate classrooms. Within these blocks, students are expected to read; be read to; to participate in shared and guided reading; to engage in shared, guided, and interactive writing; to talk to and with other students and the teacher; and to focus on words, letters, and sounds.
3. Primary grade teachers attended professional development focused on ELLs.
4. READ 180 provided additional reading support for intermediate students after school.
5. Reading Recovery for first graders—four half-time teachers.
6. Two literacy coaches on staff, one for primary and the other for intermediate grades.
7. Support for struggling readers in pull-out work with literacy coaches during the school day, in addition to in-class reading instruction.

Howard Elementary typically enrolls about 600 students each year. Of these students about 68% are Hispanic, 11% are Asian or Pacific Islander, 9% are African American, and 10% are European American. About 87% of the students at Howard qualify for free or reduced lunch, 12% receive special education support, and 47% are identified as limited English proficient. Howard receives more money per pupil than other schools in the district. Each student at Howard has about $6,500 allocated, compared to $6,000 for other students. The school's leadership has been aggressive in seeking federal dollars and grant support to help its students.

During my 7-year study, there was one change of principals. During the second-grade year, a new principal, Mr. Morris came to the school. He was an experienced principal, especially with high-poverty schools, placed at this school to help with student achievement and to improve faculty morale. One of his first decisions was to get support for students who struggled with reading beyond first grade. He also spent numerous hours visiting classrooms, so that he could see firsthand how teachers were supporting their students in literacy learning. He worked diligently to bring parents to the school. By the end of his tenure in 2004, 87% of parents participated in school activities. And importantly, student achievement had risen, so that the school was no longer on the state's "needs improvement" list.

The majority of teachers at Howard had several years of teaching experience. About 60% had more than 2 years of experience, with 57% of these teachers falling into the range of 3–10 years. All of the teachers met the "highly qualified" expectation for elementary teachers, 40% held master's degrees, and several teachers had National Board certification. Teachers worked together in whole-school professional development, and there were grade level meetings each week. Several of the intermediate teams worked with all of the students in a grade level, where each teacher taught a different level of readers and was responsible for a single content area, such as science or social studies.

Students at Howard Elementary benefited from state regulations that required reduced class size in the primary grades. In first through third grade, there were approximately 15–17 children in each classroom. Because of a limited number of classrooms, there were many team teaching situations in the primary grades, so in practice, a room might have 30 students but two full-time teachers responsible for them. In the intermediate grades, the size of each class grew larger, with approximately 25 children in each classroom with a single teacher. The teachers also benefited from numerous instructional aides assigned to them, and ESL teachers and aides were available as well.

The Students

During the first week of kindergarten, students were individually assessed by their teachers. I met with the parents while their child was being assessed and secured 16 children for this study. Three children who left the school during kindergarten or first grade were discontinued from the study. Because so many of the parents, particularly the mothers, spoke only Spanish, I had a bilingual aide help me explain the purpose of my study. She facilitated conversations in which parents described their child's home literacy experiences.

I selected children who represented the demographics of the school and I balanced gender. Table 1.1 presents an overview of the focal children and a few of their experiences.

Of these children, eight were of Hispanic origin (seven came from Mexico and one from El Salvador), one was Filipino, one was Native American, one was black, and two were European American. Of the 10 children who were ELLs, none had preschool experience. Kindergarten was their first formal school experience.

TABLE 1.1 Overview of Focal Children

Name	Home language	Preschool experience	Home literacy practices
Anthony	English	Yes	Mom frequently reads to him, and he follows the words.
Bonnie	Spanish	No	Mom occasionally reads to her.
Calvin	English	Yes	Mom occasionally reads to him.
Eric	English (Native American heritage)	Yes	Mom frequently reads to him, and he brings books from home to share at school.
Fredy	Spanish	No	No reading at home.
Heidee	Tagalog	No	Mom and Dad frequently read to her.
Jaryd	English	No	Mom occasionally reads to him.
Josie	Spanish	No	Mom occasionally reads to her.
Julio	Spanish	No	No reading at home.
Lucero	Spanish	No	Mom reads to her in Spanish.
Maria	Spanish	No	Mom and Dad occasionally read to her.
Maritza	Spanish	No	No reading at home.
Sandra	Spanish	No	Mom and Dad read to her in Spanish and English.

Collecting Data

To learn about literacy learning and instruction, I visited classrooms weekly and spent an entire morning or afternoon with the students and their teachers. I collected and copied multiple samples of students' work, and I often wrote down conversations they had with other students or their teacher. Frequently, I also wrote down snippets of their reading and the titles of the books they read in reading group or independently.

I interviewed teachers more formally at the beginning and end of each school year. Also, I chatted with them on each visit and asked them to inform me of the literacy learning of the focal students. At the end of each year, I interviewed students and often invited them to participate in informal assessment of their word knowledge (Bear et al., 2004), and to draw and write about themselves. (For more fine-grained details of the study's data collection and analysis see the Appendix.)

FINAL THOUGHTS

From this beginning, I entered Howard Elementary School to follow a small group of focal students for 7 years. In the following chapters, I share information about the children's literacy learning and instruction. Beyond this focus, I describe the students as individuals and how they maneuvered within their classrooms, and also look closely at a few exemplary teachers and how they met the needs of their students in extraordinary ways. The stories of these children, their teachers, and their school provide opportunities for others who are involved with similar children in high-poverty schools to learn about ways to support student learning, about obstacles to learning, and about the importance of teachers in children's learning.

REFERENCES

Adams, M. (1990). *Beginning to read: Thinking and learning about print.* Cambridge, MA: MIT Press.
Alexander, K., & Entwisle, D. (1996). Schools and children at risk. In A. Booth

& J. Dunn (Eds.), *Family and school links: How do they affect educational outcomes?* (pp. 67–88). Mahwah, NJ: Erlbaum.

Allington, R. (1984). Content, coverage, and contextual reading in reading groups. *Journal of Reading Behavior, 16*, 85–96.

Allington, R., & Johnston, P. (2002). *Reading to learn: Lessons from exemplary fourth-grade classrooms.* New York: Guilford Press.

Allington, R., & Walmsley, S. (Eds.). (1995). *No quick fix: Rethinking literacy programs in America's elementary schools.* New York: Teachers College Press.

Anderson, R., Wilson, P., & Fielding, L. (1988). Growth in reading and how children spend their time outside of school. *Reading Research Quarterly, 23*, 285–303.

Bear, D., Invernizzi, M., Templeton, S., & Johnston, F. (2004). *Words their way: Word study for phonics, vocabulary, and spelling instruction* (3rd ed.). Upper Saddle River, NJ: Prentice-Hall.

Beykont, Z. (2002). Introduction. In Z. Beykont (Ed.), *The power of culture* (pp. vii–xxxvi). Cambridge, MA: Harvard Education Publishing.

Block, C. C., & Mangieri, J. N. (2003). *Exemplary literacy teachers: Promoting success for all children in grades K–5.* New York: Guilford Press.

Cleary, B. (1988). *A girl from Yamhill.* New York: Morrow.

Cummins, J. (2003). Reading and the bilingual student: Fact and fiction. In G. Garcia (Ed.), *English learners: Reading the highest level of English literacy* (pp. 2–33). Newark, DE: International Reading Association.

Cunningham, A., & Stanovich, K. (1998). Early reading acquisition and its relation to reading experience and ability 10 years later. *Developmental Psychology 33*, 934–945.

Delpit, L. (1995). *Other people's children: Cultural conflict in the classroom.* New York: New Press.

Dillon, D. (2000). *Reconsidering how to meet the literacy needs of all students.* Newark, DE: International Reading Association.

Dyson, A. (2001). Writing and children's symbolic repertoires: Development unhinged. In S. B. Neuman & D. K. Dickinson (Eds.), *Handbook of early literacy research* (Vol. 1, pp. 126–141). New York: Guilford Press.

Dyson, A., & Genishi, C. (2005). *On the case: Approaches to language and literacy research.* New York: Teachers College Press and NCRELL.

Fillmore, L. (1997). *Authentic literature in ESL instruction.* Glenview, IL: Scott Foresman.

Garcia, E. (2000). Bilingual children's reading. In M. Kamil, P. Mosenthal, P.D. Pearson, & R. Barr (Eds.), *Handbook of reading research* (Vol. III, pp. 813–834). Mahwah, NJ: Erlbaum.

Graves, M. (2000). A vocabulary program to complement and bolster a middle-grade comprehension program. In B. Taylor, M. Graves., & P. van den

Broek (Eds.), *Reading for meaning* (pp. 116–135). New York: Teachers College Press.

Gutierrez, K. (2001). What's new in the English language arts: Challenging policies and practices. *Language Arts, 78,* 564–569.

Gutierrez, K., Basquedano-Lopez, P., & Turner, M. (1997). Putting language back into language arts: When the radical middle meets the third space. *Language Arts, 74,* 368–378.

Hart, B., & Risley, T. (1999). *The social world of children learning to talk.* Baltimore: Brookes.

Hiebert, E., Pearson, P., Taylor, B., Richardson, V., & Paris, S. (1997). *Every child a reader.* Ann Arbor: CIERA/University of Michigan.

Juel, C. (1988). Learning to read and write: A longitudinal study of 54 children from first through fourth grades. *Journal of Educational Psychology, 80,* 437–447.

Juel, C. (1994). *Learning to read and write in one elementary school.* New York: Springer-Verlag.

Knapp, M. (1995). *Teaching for meaning in high-poverty classrooms.* New York: Teachers College Press.

Ladson-Billings, G. (1994). *The dreamkeepers: Successful teachers of African American children.* San Francisco: Jossey-Bass.

McDermott, R. (1977). The cultural context of learning to read. In S. F. Wanat (Ed.), *Papers in applied linguistics* (pp. 10–18). Arlington, VA: Center for Applied Linguistics.

McGee, L. M., & Richgels, D. J. (2003). *Designing early literacy programs: Strategies for at-risk preschool and kindergarten children.* New York: Guilford Press.

Moll, L., & Diaz, S. (1987). Change as the goal of educational research. *Anthropology and Education Quarterly, 18,* 300–311.

National Reading Panel. (2000). *Teaching children to read: An evidence-based assessment of the scientific research literature on reading and its implications for reading instruction: Reports of the subgroups.* Washington, DC: National Institute of Child Health and Human Development.

Neufeld, P., & Fitzgerald, J. (2001). Early English reading development: Latino English learners in the "low" reading group. *Research in the Teaching of English, 36,* 64–105.

Nieto, S. (1999). *The light in their eyes: Creating multicultural learning communities.* New York: Teachers College Press.

Pressley, M. (1998). *Reading instruction that works: The case for balanced teaching.* New York: Guilford Press.

Pressley, M., Rankin, J., & Yokoi, L. (1996). A survey of instructional practices of primary grade teachers nominated as effective in promoting literacy. *Elementary School Journal, 96,* 363–384.

Pressley, M., Wharton-McDonald, R., Mistretta-Hampston, J., & Echevarria,

M. (1998). Literacy instruction in 10 grade fourth- and fifth-grade class-rooms in upstate New York. *Scientific Study of Reading, 2,* 159–194.

Raphael, T. (2000). Balancing literature and instruction: Lessons from the Book Club project. In B. Taylor, M. Graves, & P. van den Broek (Eds.), *Reading for meaning* (pp. 70–94). New York: Teachers College Press.

Rasinski, T. (2004). *Assessing reading fluency.* Honolulu, HI: Pacific Resources for Education and Learning.

Reglin, G. (1995). *Achievement for African-American students: Strategies for the diverse classroom.* Bloomington, IN: National Educational Service.

Share, D., Jorm A., MacLean, R., & Mathews, R. (1984). Sources of individual differences in reading achievement. *Journal of Educational Psychology, 76,* 1309–1324.

Snow, C., Barnes, W., Chandler, J., Goodman, I., & Hemphill, L. (1991). *Unfulfilled expectations: Home and school influences on literacy.* Cambridge, MA: Harvard University Press.

Snow, C., Burns, M., & Griffin, P. (1998). *Preventing reading difficulties in young children.* Washington, DC: National Academy Press.

Stanovich, K. (1986). Matthew effects in reading: Some consequences of individual differences in the acquisition of literacy. *Reading Research Quarterly, 21,* 360–406.

Stanovich, K. (1993). Romance and reality. *Reading Teacher, 47,* 280–291.

Tabors, P. O., & Snow, C. E. (2001). Young bilingual children and early literacy development. In S. B. Neuman & D. K. Dickinson (Eds.), *Handbook of early literacy research* (Vol. 1, pp. 159–178). New York: Guilford Press.

Taylor, B., Pearson, P.D., Clark, K., & Walpole, S. (1999). Effective schools/accomplished teachers. *Reading Teacher, 53,* 156–159.

Torgeson, J., & Davis, C. (1996). Individual difference variables that predict response to training in phonological awareness. *Journal of Experimental Child Psychology, 63,* 1–21.

Yopp, H.K., & Yopp, R.H. (2000). Supporting phonemic awareness development in the classroom. *Reading Teacher, 54,* 130–143.

Chapter 2

Looking at Students' Literacy Learning

> Ramona thought growing up was the slowest thing there
> was, slower even than waiting for Christmas to come.
> She had been waiting years just to get to kindergarten,
> and the last half hour was the slowest part of all.
> —BEVERLY CLEARY (1968, p. 14)

In this quote, Ramona shares her thinking as she entered her first day of kindergarten. For Ramona, just getting to kindergarten took forever, and getting there was the most important part. I am sure that the children in my study had similar feelings as they entered kindergarten, particularly those who had older brothers and sisters, and were more familiar with formal schooling. I also shared Ramona's feelings as I began my study, for I knew that I would spend 7 years with a small group of students as I followed their literacy learning trajectories. It seemed to me that it took forever to get everything in place to begin the study, and finally I was nervously at the doorstep for my first visit.

LITERACY GROWTH BY GRADE LEVEL

Our journey began when the students entered kindergarten and ended when they graduated from sixth grade and would begin a new
(*text continues on p. 33*)

TABLE 2.1. Overview of End-of-the-Year Literacy Learning

Names and home language	End of kindergarten	End of first grade	End of second grade	End of third grade	End of fourth grade	End of fifth grade	End of sixth grade
Anthony (English)	At grade level Able to track memorized text Uses book language to retell stories Sound–symbol (Mrs. Martin & Mrs. George)	Below grade level, level 13 Letter Name Relies on predictable text (Mrs. Cullen & Mrs. Adams)	At grade level, level 21 Within Word Reading chapter books (Mrs. Scott & Mrs. Ford)	Above grade level, level 25 Syllable Juncture Terra Nova— 37% reading 37% vocabulary 38% reading composite (Ms. Read)	Above grade level Derivational Constancy CRT—72% in reading Terra Nova— 70% reading 38% vocabulary 55% reading composite No writing assessment (Mrs. Chew)	Above grade level Derivational Constancy CRT—72.5% in reading SRI—Lexile 810 (6th grade) (Mrs. Katen)	Above grade level Syllable Juncture CRT—82.5% in reading Writing—I-4, O-4, C-4, V-4 SRI—Lexile 950 (8th grade) (Ms. Jones)
Bonnie (Spanish)	Below grade level Recognizes x Looks at books (Mrs. Harter)	Below grade level, level 12 Letter Name Relies on predictable text Reading Recovery (Mrs. Cullen & Mrs. Adams)	At grade level, level 21 Within Word Reading simple novels (Mrs. Scott & Mrs. Ford)	Below grade level Syllable Juncture Terra Nova— 17% reading 16% vocabulary 16% reading composite (Mrs. Walker)	At grade level Derivational Constancy CRT—45% in reading Terra Nova— 6% reading 25% vocabulary 14% reading composite Writing— I-1.5, O-1.5, C-3, V-2.5 (Mrs. Scott)	At or slightly below grade level Derivational Constancy CRT—45% in reading SRI—Lexile 874 (7th grade) (Mrs. Katen)	Moved to a charter school

Calvin (English)	Below grade level Recognizes most letters, except *t* and *y* Looks at books (Mrs. Harter)	At grade level, level 16 Letter Name Relies on predictable text Reading Recovery (Mrs. Cullen & Mrs. Adams)	Below grade level, level 14 Letter Name (Mrs. Stewart & Mrs. Harrison)	Below grade level (early 2nd) Within Word Terra Nova— 15% reading 47% vocabulary 29% reading composite (Mrs. Walker)	At grade level Syllable Juncture CRT—65% in reading Terra Nova— 31% reading 27% vocabulary 29% reading composite Writing—I-2.5, O-1.5, C-2.5, V-3 (Mrs. Spears)	Below grade level Derivational Constancy CRT—65% in reading SRI—Lexile 615 (4th grade) (Mr. Bussoni)	Moved to a charter school
Eric (English)	Above grade level Sound–symbol Uses book language to retell stories Able to read predictable text (Mrs. Martin & Mrs. George)	At grade level, level 17 Within Word Independent reader Developing fluency (Mrs. Messina & Mrs. Denton)	Above grade level, level 28 Syllable Juncture (Mrs. Stevens & Mrs. Smith)	Above grade level Syllable Juncture Terra Nova— 40% reading 35% vocabulary 38% reading composite (Mrs. Erin)	Above grade level Derivational Constancy CRT—67.5% in reading Terra Nova— 58% reading 67% vocabulary 63% reading composite Writing—I-2.5, O-3, C-3.5, V-2.5 (Mrs. Scott)	At grade level Derivational Constancy CRT—67.5% in reading SRI—Lexile 629 (4th grade) (Mr. Bussoni)	Above grade level Derivational Constancy CRT—60% in reading SRI—Lexile 777 (5th grade) Writing—I-3, O-3, C-3, V-3.5 (Ms. Jones)

(*continued*)

TABLE 2.1. (*continued*)

Names amd home language	End of kindergarten	End of first grade	End of second grade	End of third grade	End of fourth grade	End of fifth grade	End of sixth grade
Fredy (Spanish)	Below grade level Recognizes *f* Looks at books Spanish dominant (Mrs. Harter)	Below grade level, level 12 Letter Name Relies on predictable text (Mr. Short & Mrs. Sims)	At grade level, level 21 Letter Name (Mrs. Stevens & Mrs. Smith)	At grade level Syllable Juncture IRI at 5th-grade level Terra Nova— 20% reading 13% vocabulary 16% reading composite (Mrs. Fryer)	Below grade level Derivational Constancy CRT—37% in reading Terra Nova— 21% reading 25% vocabulary 22% reading composite Writing—I-2, O-2, C-3, V-2 (Mrs. Scott)	Below grade level Derivational Constancy Moved in October	
Heidee (Tagalog)	Above grade level Sound–symbol Uses oral language to retell stories Able to memorize predictable text (Mrs. Harter)	Above grade level, level 20 Letter Name Independent reader Developing fluency (Mrs. Kirby & Ms. Mears)	Above grade level, level 25 Within Word (Mrs. Scott & Mrs. Ford)	Above grade level Syllable Juncture 7th grade IRI independent Terra Nova— 30% reading 45% vocabulary 38% reading composite (Mrs. Fryer)	Above grade level Derivational Constancy CRT—75% in reading Terra Nova— 51% reading 43% vocabulary 51% reading composite Writing—I-3, O-3.5, C-3, V-4 (Mrs. Scott)	Moved	

Jaryd (English)	Below grade level Recognizes *i* Looks at books (Mrs. Harter)	At grade level, level 17 Letter Name Relies on predictable text Reading Recovery (Mr. Shott & Mrs. Sims)	Below grade level, level 18 Within Word Beginning fluency (Mrs. Stevens & Mrs. Smith)	Below grade level Within Word Going to summer school and university clinic Terra Nova— 21% reading 30% vocabulary 15% reading composite (Mrs. Erin)	Below grade level Syllable Juncture CRT—30% in reading Terra Nova— 2% reading 6% vocabulary 3% reading composite Writing—I-1, O-1, C-1, V-1 (Mrs. Chew)	Below grade level Syllable Juncture CRT—30% in reading SRI—Lexile 514 (3rd grade) (Mr. Bussoni)
						Below grade level Syllable Juncture CRT—45% in reading Writing—I-2, O-1.5, C-1.5, V-1.5 SRI—Lexile 623 (4th grade) (Mr. McGuire)
Josie (Spanish)	Below grade level Recognizes some letters; *e, s, l, n, o,* and *i* Looks at books (Mrs. Martin & Mrs. George)	Above grade level, level 20 Letter Name Independent reader (Mr. Shott & Mrs. Sims)	At grade level, level 21 Within Word Fluent reader (Mrs. Scott & Mrs. Ford)	At grade level Syllable Juncture Terra Nova— 44% reading 25% vocabulary 34% reading composite (Mrs. Erin)	At grade level Syllable Juncture CRT—67% in reading Terra Nova— 66% reading 46% vocabulary 56% reading composite Writing—I-3.5, O-4, C-4.5, V-4.5 (Mrs. Spears)	At grade level Derivational Constancy CRT—67.5% in reading SRI—Lexile 685 (4th grade) (Mrs. Callep)
						At grade level Derivational Constancy CRT—70% in reading Writing—I-3.5, O-3, C-3, V-4.5 SRI—Lexile 815 (6th grade) IRI—independent at 6th grade (Ms. Booth)

(continued)

TABLE 2.1. (*continued*)

Names amd home language	End of kindergarten	End of first grade	End of second grade	End of third grade	End of fourth grade	End of fifth grade	End of sixth grade
Julio (Spanish)	Below grade level Recognizes some letters; c, j, p, m Looks at books (Mrs. Harter)	Below grade level, level 12 Letter Name Relies on predictable text Reading Recovery (Mrs. Messina & Mrs. Denton)	Below grade level, level 14 Letter Name (Mrs. Stevens & Mrs. Smith)	Below grade level (2.8 STAR) Within Word Terra Nova—7% math (Ms. Read)	At grade level Syllable Juncture CRT—47% in reading IRI—independent at 4th grade (on Ritalin) Terra Nova— 21% reading 18% vocabulary 19% reading composite No writing assessment (Mrs. Chew)	Below grade level. Syllable Juncture CRT—47.5% in reading SRI—Lexile 432 (2nd grade) Summer school After school reading program, Read 180 (Mrs. Katen)	Below grade level Syllable Juncture CRT—67.5% in reading Writing—I-2.5, C-2.5, O-2.5, V-3 SRI—Lexile 498 (3rd grade) Daily support with reading specialist (Mr. McGuire)

Lucero (Spanish)	Below grade level Recognizes most letters except u, v, w, and y Uses oral language to retell stories in Spanish and English Uses book language for retelling (Mrs. Martin & Mrs. George)	At grade level, level 17 Letter Name Relies on predictable text (Mr. Shott & Mrs. Sims)	Above grade level, level 24 Within Word (Mrs. Stewart & Mrs. Harrison)	At grade level Derivational Constancy Terra Nova— 45% reading 59% vocabulary 55% reading composite (Mrs. Walker)	At grade level Derivational Constancy CRT—65% in reading Terra Nova— 42% reading 32% vocabulary 38% reading composite Writing—1-3.5, O-3.5, C-3.5, V-3.5 (Mrs. Spears)	At grade level Derivational Constancy CRT—65% in reading SRI—Lexile 805 (6th grade) (Mr. Bussoni)	At grade level Derivational Constancy CRT—75% in reading Writing—1-3.5, O-3.5, C-3, V-3 SRI—Lexile 846 (6th grade) IRI—independent at 6th grade (Ms. Booth)
Maria (Spanish)	At grade level Sound–symbol Oral language for retelling (Mrs. Harter)	Above grade level, level 20 Letter Name Independent reader Developing fluency (Mr. Shott & Mrs. Sims)	At grade level, level 21 Within Word (Mrs. Stewart & Mrs. Harrison)	At grade level Syllable Juncture Terra Nova— 42% reading 34% vocabulary 46% reading composite (Mrs. Walker)	At grade level Derivational Constancy CRT—67% in reading Terra Nova— 50% reading 22% vocabulary 36% reading composite Writing—1-2, O-3, C-2.5, V-3 (Mrs. Chew)	At grade level Derivational Constancy CRT—67.5% in reading SRI—Lexile 744 (5th grade) (Mr. Bussoni)	Above grade level Derivational Constancy CRT—70% in reading Writing—1-3, O-3, C-3.5, V-3 SRI—Lexile 977 (8th grade) (Ms. Jones)

(continued)

TABLE 2.1. (continued)

Names and home language	End of kindergarten	End of first grade	End of second grade	End of third grade	End of fourth grade	End of fifth grade	End of sixth grade
Maritza (Spanish)	Below grade level Recognizes some letters; b, m, p, t, and a Looks at books (Mrs. Martin & Mrs. George)	Below grade level, level 14 Letter Name Relies on predictable texts Reading Recovery (Mrs. Cullen & Mrs. Adams)	Above grade level, level 24 Within Word Starts 2nd grade in Mexico (until end of September) (Mrs. Stevens & Mrs. Smith)	At grade level, level 21 Within Word Terra Nova— 35% reading 33% vocabulary 35% reading composite (Ms. Read)	At grade level Syllable Juncture CRT—67% in reading Terra Nova— 60% reading 37% vocabulary 49% reading composite Writing—I-2.5, O-2.5, C-3.5, V-3 (Mrs. Spears)	At grade level Derivational Constancy CRT—67.5% in reading SRI—Lexile 715 (5th grade) (Mrs. Callep)	Above grade level Derivational Constancy CRT—62.5% in reading Writing—I-4, O-4, C-3, V-4 SRI—Lexile 681 (4th grade) (Ms. Jones)
Sandra (Spanish)	Below grade level Recognizes most letters, except u and w Looks at books (Mrs. Martin & Mrs. George)	Below grade level, level 14 Within Word Relies on predictable text Reading Recovery (Mrs. Kirby & Ms. Mears)	Above grade level, level 27 Within Word Mrs. Stevens & Mrs. Smith	Above grade level Syllable Juncture IRI— independent at 7th grade Terra Nova— 48% reading 23% vocabulary 35% reading composite (Mrs. Fryer)	At grade level Derivational Constancy CRT—62% in reading Terra Nova— 37% reading 21% vocabulary 29% reading composite Writing—I-2.5, O-2.5, C-3, V-2.5 (Mrs. Chew)	Above grade level Derivational Constancy CRT—62.5% in reading SRI—Lexile 892 (7th grade) (Mrs. Katen)	Above grade level Derivational Constancy CRT—87.5% in reading (In Mexico for writing assessment) SRI—Lexile 919 (8th grade) (Mr. McGuire)

Notes. CRT, criterion-referenced test; IRI, Informal Reading Inventory; SRI, Scholastic Reading Inventory. Text gradient guide (Reading Recovery levels): first grade—level 16; second grade—level 20; third grade—levels 21, 22; fourth grade—levels 21, 25; fifth grade—level 27; sixth grade—levels 29, 20. Writing assessment abbreviations: I, ideas; O, organization; C, conventions; V, voice.

adventure in middle school. The majority of this chapter describes students' literacy growth as they moved from grade to grade. Table 2.1 provides an overview of end-of-the-year accomplishments for each student. It can be used as a guide when viewing the students and their yearly progress. I end the chapter with an overview of their learning throughout elementary school. Throughout this and other chapters, there will be more extensive explorations of individual students, shared in longer sections when they are featured.

Kindergarten

"Well . . . uh . . . you said if I sat here I would get a present," said Ramona at last, "but you didn't say how long I had to sit here."

If Miss Binney had looked puzzled before, she now looked baffled. "Ramona, I don't understand—" she began.

"Yes, you did," said Ramona, nodding. "You told me to sit here for the present, and I have been sitting here ever since school started and you haven't given me a present."

—BEVERLY CLEARY (1968, pp. 26–27)

Vocabulary confused Ramona on her first day of kindergarten, and she came to school speaking English. Her difficulty involved the word *present;* she understood it to mean a gift, but the teacher was using it as a time marker. At Howard Elementary, very few children came with a home language of English; for most, the school's language was unfamiliar. The majority of these children would not have understood even one meaning for the word *present.*

Kindergarten, unlike other grades at Howard, began with an individual assessment of each child. During the first week of school, the children participated in a kindergarten screening used to determine readiness for kindergarten instruction. This assessment emphasized language; children had to complete sentences or provide the correct form of a word, singular or plural, present or past tense, for example. There were also questions dealing with visual–motor coordination, drawing, name writing, and gross motor development. For many of these children, this assessment was troublesome because it was only given in English. Many parents attempted to help their children as they participated in this assessment. The result was that all parties were frustrated—the teachers, because they were only allowed to give the assessment in English; the children, because they did not understand the words of the teachers; and the parents, who understood the expectations but were not allowed to help their children.

The focal children's scores on this initial screening ranged from a low of 0 to a high of 26. (The highest possible score was 36.) The kindergarten teachers informed me that "most children in this school score in the 20s." Of the three focal children who scored the lowest, one was English dominant (Jaryd), and the others were Spanish dominant (Julio and Maritza). It was interesting that Jaryd scored so low (9), because he understood the language of the teacher and the majority of the assessment was language based. His mother informed his teacher that "Jaryd never held a pencil, used scissors, wrote, or colored at home." Jaryd struggled with all of the small motor skills required in this assessment, and these struggles were represented by his low score.

The following scores were earned by the focal children: Anthony (26), Lucero and Eric (22), Maria (20), Calvin and Sandra (19), Fredy and Heidee (17), Josie (15), Bonnie (14), and Maritza and Jaryd (9); Julio refused to participate. When scanning these scores, there is no relationship between a score and home language. Of the six top-scoring children, three have English as a home language, and for the other three, English is a new language. I wondered how these scores on the initial screening would impact instruction.

It was interesting that this assessment followed the old tradition of reading readiness. None of the major predictors of academic success were included, with the exception of name writing. The children were never asked to recognize alphabet letters or their sounds, and there was no phonological awareness screening, knowledge that is highly predictive of school success (National Reading Panel, 2000; Snow, Burns, & Griffin, 1998; Yopp & Yopp, 2000).

After this first week of screening, kindergarten began. When I arrived on the first day, there was bedlam outside of the classrooms as parents, friends, and younger children all gathered to send a child to kindergarten. When the children crossed the threshold of their classroom, many parents continued to look through the windows as their child participated in the first activities of kindergarten. The teachers began their day by taking attendance; however, few children responded when their names were called. They just looked at their teacher with big bright eyes, not understanding that they were to say "here" when their names were called.

There were two kindergarten rooms that children attended and two sessions of kindergarten in each room—morning and afternoon. While the teachers welcomed separate classrooms, there was not sufficient space in the school for stand-alone classrooms. The teachers solved this problem by separating one room with a divider of material boxes and cabinets. Importantly, although the room was physically separated, the noise was incredible, because there were typically 50 children in attendance in both rooms.

Although I detail in Chapter 3 the instruction provided to these children, most of the instruction they received was in phonics. They were taught letters and their accompanying sounds for the majority of the day. Teachers rarely grouped students for individualized or small-group instruction based on students' strengths or needs. And so the answer to my query about how the initial screening would inform instruction was answered—it did not.

The children began the year with very disparate knowledge of literacy and of English, the language of the school. They ended the year with wide discrepancies in their literacy knowledge and understanding. Although the instruction was the same for all students in a classroom, some students who came to school with much literacy knowledge, such as Calvin and Lucero, did not end the year demonstrating academic success. Other students, such as Jaryd and Julio, ended the year with little additional literacy knowledge that was valued in school.

Letter Knowledge, Sound–Symbol Knowledge, and Name Writing

At the end of kindergarten, Heidee, Maria, Anthony, and Eric demonstrated complete knowledge of letters and some understanding of sound–symbol relationships. For example, Anthony was asked to spell *bed, ship, drive, bump,* and *when* (see Figure 2.1). Anthony provided a full phonemic representation of each word, because there was an initial and final consonant with a vowel for each representation. He substituted an *a* for the short *e* in *bed*, a common substitu-

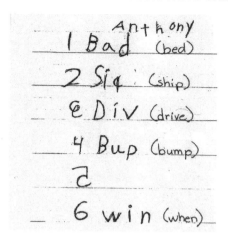

FIGURE 2.1. Anthony's spelling in kindergarten.

tion (see Bear, Invernizzi, Templeton, & Johnston, 2004). He used the *s* in *ship* to represent the digraph /sh/ and a *w* in *when* to represent the /wh/ digraph. He neglected to represent the *r* in *drive*, and he used the letter *i* to represent the long sound of /ī/. Although his representations of these words were not correct, they demonstrated his knowledge of letters and their corresponding sounds.

Calvin, Lucero, and Sandra recognized the majority of alphabet letters, although they did not connect sounds to them. Maritza, Jaryd, Josie, Julio, Bonnie, and Fredy recognized fewer than 10 alphabet letters. For these children, there were connections between home language and letter knowledge, although, perhaps surprisingly, they were not linear. Heidee and Maria, who understood sound–symbol relationships at the end of the year, came to school with a home language that was not English (Heidee: Tagalog; Maria: Spanish). Of the children who recognized most alphabet letters, Lucero and Sandra had Spanish as a home language. Of the children who knew the fewest alphabet letters, five had a home language of Spanish. Thus, home language was not directly related to letter knowledge, although the majority of children with a paucity of letter knowledge also had a home language other than English.

The variability in letter knowledge is puzzling, because the teachers emphasized this knowledge throughout the year. However, when students were assessed in May, they could not display this knowledge without extensive scaffolding from their teachers. For example, the only way that Bonnie recognized *x* was when her teacher removed the other letters from sight and showed her a picture of an X-ray.

Coupled with most students' lack of alphabet recognition was their inability to write letters, particularly when they were expected to write the initial consonant in a word. They also had great difficulty orally supplying words that began with a particular consonant. For example, Calvin offered the word *dog* when the teacher asked for a word beginning with *b*. When students came up with a correct word, it was through trial and error.

In addition to letter and sound knowledge, students were asked to write their names. By the end of the year, the majority of focal children wrote their first names correctly and automatically. Fredy and Jaryd were the only two who found this task difficult and laborious. Fredy wrote his name as FRBPIE. These letters are similar to some of the letters in his name. Jaryd appeared to use a letter string that included *F, T, A,* and *P.* Examples from his name writing include FTAP or FTPA. Unlike Fredy, these letters, other than the *A,* do not appear in his name.

The only other writing in which children engaged was copying from the board. Teachers wrote words on the board related to an alphabet letter, such as *bear* for *b,* and children copied the word and picture. This task was difficult, because they had to look at the board for every letter that they copied. When I watched this, I could see their heads go up and down for each letter. They were unable to copy an entire word, and they could not read these words without picture support. The children never wrote in journals or about the books that were read to them during the year.

Oral Language

From the first day of school, children were taught, and were expected to respond, in English. The children tried to stay attentive, but those who were learning English frequently stopped paying attention to the instruction. They talked quietly to children next to them in Spanish or just looked around the room. Gee (1985, 1990) noted that when students do not share the language of the teacher, their participation in learning activities is difficult. A specific example of this comes from Julio's behavior throughout the year. Whenever his teacher taught or read, he disappeared to the bathroom or to the sink to wash his hands. When students were dispersed to small groups, he reappeared, joined a group, and copied whatever they were doing.

During direct instruction, children were expected to respond with a correct answer to each question posed by the teacher. For example, on one occasion, the teacher was reading *If You Give a Mouse a Cookie* (Numeroff, 1985) and when done, she asked the children to tell her what things the mouse wanted. One child said, "Cookie." Then she asked another child, who repeated, "Cookie." When the third child gave the same answer, she moved the children to another activity. This type of interaction was common throughout the year. Unfortunately, this limited language use by children has been documented as common in other classrooms with culturally and linguistically diverse students (Ramirez, Yuen, Ramey, & Pasta, 1991). Although this is a typical way that teachers interact with ELLs, learning is not a passive activity (Bruner, 1999; Cole & Wertsch, 1996; Gee, 2002). Therefore, these students did not have the opportunity to use language to learn about language or the content that was presented.

Each morning, as children arrived, they looked at books. Frequently, they showed an illustration to a neighboring child and talked about it. For example, Josie loved to share illustrations, particularly if they were of monsters. She enjoyed making pretend monster noises. Therefore, there were unofficial conversations about books; however, there were few official conversations about books shared with teachers. Children passively listened to teachers read, then completed phonics activities that were to be correctly done. They had little chance to talk about their learning or about the interesting errors they made in completing learning activities (Marshall, 1992).

On most occasions, children were quiet, because they were expected to listen to the teacher and then work silently on assigned tasks. However, when working at tables, they whispered to each other in Spanish, English, or a combination of both. The children implicitly knew the home languages of other children and adapted their conversations to the children near them. For example, Spanish was spoken if all the children knew Spanish. If an English-dominant child was at the table, children moved from Spanish to English to ensure understanding.

At the end of the year, all the children, regardless of home language, had not acquired academic language. They responded with a single word to teachers' questions, but they never engaged in extended conversations centered on learning. Children such as Sandra and Julio never participated in English conversations. They only talked informally with their friends in Spanish; thus, they never acquired conversational or academic English.

Book Reading and Book Knowledge

As described earlier, the major time children engaged with books was when they entered the classroom. If I listened in to children's pretend reading, I learned that they most often used oral language to retell a story (Sulzby, 1985). If they had not heard the story before, they just labeled the illustrations on a page, and every page was a separate event, because there were no connections across pages to form a story. Few experimented with book language, such as "Once upon a time" or "The End." The only children who used book language when retelling a story were Anthony, Eric, and Lucero. Although they used book language, they were not able to point to a specific word when asked. Anthony, on occasion, ran his hand under a line of print on a page.

The children pointed to the front and back of a book, turned pages correctly, and recognized the top and bottom of a book page. They focused on illustrations and were not aware that words were important in carrying the message.

Summary of Kindergarten Literacy Learning

The children developed tentative understandings about reading and writing. They enjoyed looking through books and chatting about

illustrations with friends. A few fully understood sound–symbol relationships, many recognized alphabet letters, and several knew fewer
than five alphabet letters. Most of the children needed to develop understanding of the importance of words in books, phonemic awareness, and phonics skills. They also required opportunities to engage
in conversations about books in which they could learn about the literal and inferential understandings related to them. Finally, they
needed opportunities to write, when they were not just expected to
copy but to convey a message that was personally meaningful to
them.

When I asked children to tell me about kindergarten, one
comment was repeated: "I really didn't know what they meant."
Children said this in different ways, but they focused on not gaining
meaning from teachers' instruction. The other dominant comment
was about not knowing how to read or write—"I couldn't read," "I
couldn't write good," and "I didn't read at all. I remember that."

First Grade

Workbooks were collected. Reading circles were next. Prepared
to attack words, Ramona limped to a little chair in the front of
the room with the rest of her reading group. . . . The reading
group was more interesting now that her group was attacking
bigger words. Fire engine. Ramona read to herself and thought,
Pow! I got you, fire engine.
                                        —BEVERLY CLEARY (1975, p. 187)

Similar to Ramona, the children in first grade learned about reading
groups and about attacking words. Although there were differences
in grouping in first grade (small groups were used as well as whole
group), teachers continued the focus on phonics and word attack, be-
lieving that these skills were the most critical for young students.
Comprehension specific strategies were infrequently focused upon
during small-group instruction in first grade.

The children entered four first-grade classrooms. Each room had
a pair of teachers because there were too few rooms in the school to
meet the state-mandated smaller class size for first grade. One of
these rooms was also a combination first- and second-grade class,

again in response to the numbers of children rather than to a curricular plan.

All of the first-grade teachers put students into ability groupings for reading instruction. In three of the rooms, teachers utilized guided- and shared-reading strategies for instruction. Children chorally read once they had performed a picture walk of leveled text. They also had phonics instruction focused on sound–symbol relationships. In one room, reading instruction was predominantly independent reading. For more explicit instruction, the class was broken into two groups in which they explored basal stories. More details of instruction are shared in Chapter 3.

Reading

As a group, the children became proficient as decoders by the end of first grade. They learned what was taught, which was to decode text with few oral miscues. There were few conversations about the meaning of stories during the year. Three children (Josie, Maria, and Heidee) read leveled text beyond the end of grade-level expectation of level 16. All of these children came to school with a home language other than English. This result is quite surprising, because there was no special instruction to help these children bridge their home language with the school's language, and they did not qualify for Reading Recovery support. Four children (Calvin, Eric, Jaryd, and Lucero) ended the year at grade level by reading at level 16 or 17. Of this group, only Lucero came to school with Spanish as a home language. Calvin and Jaryd received Reading Recovery support, and this extra support certainly helped them attain grade-level expectancies. Six children (Bonnie, Anthony, Fredy, Julio, Maritza, and Sandra) did not meet grade-level expectations, with instructional reading levels of 14 and below. Of this group, Anthony is the only student with English as a home language. Bonnie, Julio, Maritza, and Sandra received Reading Recovery support, but it was not sufficient to help them meet grade-level expectations.

Reading Recovery support was in some ways frustrating with respect to how children were selected. Reading Recovery was only taught in English, and children who still struggled with English did not qualify. The principal decided that Julio needed this support, and she provided it, because she was Reading Recovery trained. Fredy, one of the lowest of all first graders academically, did not receive this support because of his limited English capabilities. And at this time at Howard, there were no other support programs for students who struggled. It took a new principal to put into place additional tutoring beyond first grade. Unfortunately, these children did not benefit from this additional support until the fourth grade.

Two children had particularly interesting reading growth during first grade. Anthony came to first grade with a wealth of knowledge about books, sound–symbol relationships, and phonological awareness. However, he spent most of the year off-task during independent reading. He went to the classroom library each day, selected a book—any book, then chatted with his friends. When his room was divided into two reading groups, he moved to the back and ignored the teacher's instruction. So without instruction and/or motivation to read independently, he failed to develop into a beginning reader. Fredy, on the other hand, left kindergarten unable to write his name or to converse socially in English. During first grade, he visited Mexico for 2 months in the middle of the year. Although he did not achieve grade-level expectations, he was reading at level 12 at the end of the year. He did attend school during his trip to Mexico, and this instruction may have helped him with this achievement.

Writing

Children's writing in first grade involved mainly the completion of worksheets. However, teachers asked students to write in journals in three of the first-grade classrooms.

There was great variety in the writing in journals. Fredy, for example, used the starter "I like" for all of his entries. Figure 2.2 is an example of his journal writing. Beyond revealing that he likes soccer, Fredy's development as a writer is evident. His writing is readable because he is representing most of the key phonemes in words. He is experimenting with an alternative way to spell *play:* PLEA. Here he is aware that *play* is not spelled with a single *a;* he is just unsure of which letter is needed for the long-vowel pattern.

I like to plea Sokr

FIGURE 2.2. Fredy's journal writing.

Unlike Fredy, other children engaged in conversations with their teachers in their journals. In Figure 2.3, Sandra tells her teacher about visits to her friends' homes, then responds to her teacher's question about what she did there: "Playing Barbies." Her writing shows that she can convey a message and spell most of the words correctly.

In one first-grade class, the children only had the opportunity to copy from the board. Each morning, they spent a half-hour to an hour

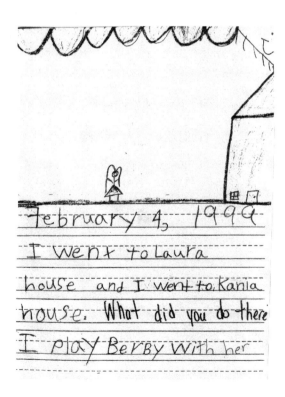

FIGURE 2.3. Sandra's journal writing.

copying a sentence or two. All of the copying exercises began with "To-day is. . . . " After this beginning, there was text about something re-lated to the day. For example, they were asked to write about a rainy day, Halloween, and so on. Calvin and Anthony approached this writ-ing in different ways. Anthony finished as quickly as he could, so that he could play with his friends in the library. Calvin got slower each day and spent almost his entire morning copying the message.

Word Study

The children spent considerable time exploring phonics skills. Al-though they came to first grade at very different points in literacy knowledge and understanding, they ended the year with similar un-derstandings about representing words. This was true for all of the focal children irrespective of home language. Typically, children rep-resented the phonemes in words, although they often confused short vowels. For example, they might spell *bed* as BAD or BID. They were unsure of digraphs. For example, they spelled *ship* as SEP or SIP. And finally, they used a single vowel to represent a long-vowel pattern. For example, they spelled *drive* as DRIV or JRIV.

Summary of First-Grade Literacy Learning

By the end of the year the children were considered to be beginning readers and writers. They could read simple text, both predictable and decodable. They conveyed simple messages in writing. They rep-resented words so that others could read them. They were more con-vergent in their learning than they had been in kindergarten or at the beginning of first grade. Unfortunately, most children still needed to learn about meaning and its connections to reading and writing.

The children talked about their accomplishments, with the ma-jority of their comments focused on words and decoding. Lucero said, "I was getting better [as a reader] because I could write more words." Sandra commented that she "learned more words." And Jaryd talked about learning to read: "I have to read one page a day. I read one and then the next. That's how I learn." Their comments re-flected the instruction provided to them. Learning to read was about learning to say the words.

Second Grade

"What did Mrs. Rogers say about me?" she demanded. . . .
"You are a good reader, but you are careless about spelling."
Ramona knew this . . . Ramona could not believe spelling was
important as long as people could understand what she meant.
                                    —BEVERLY CLEARY (1977, p. 49)

Ramona came to second grade as a confident reader, who only
needed to improve her spelling. The children at Howard did not enter second grade as confident as Ramona. They could read words,
certainly, but they were not so sure about what happened in a book.
Like Ramona, they were ready to explore more complex spellings of
words.

Similar to first grade, children entered one of four second-grade
classrooms where there were teams of teachers. These teachers
grouped students for reading instruction by ability. There were about
six reading groups in each room.

Reading

Children explored both fictional and informational text in second
grade. They moved beyond a single focus on decoding and explored
meaning. During small-group work, they often created charts to help
with understanding of informational text such as Venn diagrams or
KWL charts.

There were great shifts in literacy knowledge and understanding
related to text in second grade. Children moved from being below or
at first-grade level to being at or above second-grade level (see Table
2.2 for an overview of grade-level achievement. Grade level placement was based on teacher decisions and informal assessment). Only
three children were considered below grade level—Julio, Jaryd, and
Calvin. This was worrisome, for at the end of second grade, they still
had not achieved end-of-first-grade expectations; they were reading
at level 14 when level 16 was expected for first graders. Anthony,
Bonnie, and Fredy moved from below-grade-level to grade-level
achievement. And Eric and Lucero went from grade-level to above
grade-level expectations. Most interesting, Maritza and Sandra
showed significant growth by moving from below grade-level to

TABLE 2.2. Grade-Level Achievement

Kindergarten	First grade	Second grade	Third grade	Fourth grade	Fifth grade	Sixth grade
			Below grade level			
Bonnie	Anthony	Calvin	Bonnie	Fredy	Fredy	Julio
Calvin	Bonnie	Jaryd	Calvin	Jaryd	Julio	Jaryd
Fredy	Fredy	Julio	Jaryd		Calvin	
Jaryd	Julio		Julio		Jaryd	
Josie	Maritza					
Julio	Sandra					
Lucero						
Maritza						
Sandra						
			At grade level			
Anthony	Calvin	Anthony	Fredy	Bonnie	Bonnie	Lucero
Maria	Eric	Bonnie	Josie	Calvin	Eric	Josie
	Jaryd	Fredy	Maria	Julio	Josie	
	Lucero	Josie	Maritza	Josie	Lucero	
		Maria	Lucero	Lucero	Maria	
				Maria	Maritza	
				Maritza		
				Sandra		
			Above grade level			
Eric	Heidee	Eric	Anthony	Anthony	Sandra	Sandra
Heidee	Josie	Heidee	Eric	Eric	Anthony	Eric
	Maria	Lucero	Heidee	Heidee		Anthony
		Maritza	Sandra			Maritza
		Sandra				Maria

above grade-level expectations—a quite remarkable accomplishment for students whose home language was not English.

Complementary to grade-level achievement, students whose reading went from a low level 14 to Eric's high level 28 were considered instructional. It was common to see some children being instructed in leveled text, while others moved to chapter books. Students' instructional levels were targeted in teacher instruction.

Students also engaged in discussions centered on meaning in reading. An example of richer discussion surrounding text is shared in the following dialogue of students reading *The Rough-*

Face Girl (Martin & Shannon, 1992), a variation based on Cinderella.

> TEACHER: Who can make a prediction about this book?
>
> LUCERO: The book is about a girl with a rough face.
>
> STUDENT: She has a rough face and doesn't want to show it.
>
> TEACHER: How do you know she doesn't want to show it?
>
> STUDENT: She has her hands on her face.
>
> STUDENT: I think her sisters are mean.

This conversation continued, then students began reading. Periodically, the teacher stopped them to further their conversation about this book. What is unique to this example is that the students read silently and engaged in conversation centered on meaning. Silent reading and comprehension were not typically a focus in previous grades. Also, not all responses were directed back to the teacher, who then posed another question that was answered. Students responded to one another, before the teacher or a student asked another question.

Writing

In second grade, there was direct instruction in the conventions of writing through daily oral language (DOL) activities. Students corrected sentences with numerous errors. In addition to this instruction, they wrote in journals and were involved with process writing, during which teachers on occasion conferred with them about improving their writing.

Students' writing growth was dramatic throughout the year. The following examples from Maritza's writing demonstrate this growth:

SEPTEMBER JOURNAL ENTRY

I went to Mexico. [no corrections]

OCTOBER STORY

I have a Halloween cat and my Halloween cat has a bat on his forehead and he is going to have a cover. And make a hole on it

*so he can see when the kids come so he can scare them. So he
can say boo. [spelling corrected]*

MARCH BOOK RESPONSE ENTRY

I read about Pretty Good Magic *(Dubowski, 1987). It was so
quiet. They lived on a street called Fort Winks. One day a ma-
gician came and did magic. That night Presto put on a show.
Everyone was there. [spelling corrected]*

MAY STORY

*Once upon a time, a little Sillysaurus met a dinosaur. What is
your name? My name is Sillysaurus. Mine is too. Let's go and
play. But I need to tell my mom, OK. I will be right back.
"Mom can I go and play with my new friend?" Yes you may.
Today is your birthday. My mom said yes because today is my
birthday. So let's go and play. But we can't play for long because my family is coming. They played for a while. I need to
go now. [no corrections]*

These brief examples show how a child went from one-sentence written entries in journal writing to a variety of writings, such as stories
and responses to books being read. As the year progressed, Maritza
shared ideas in more complex ways, from multiple sentences to conversation. Her Sillysaurus story showed her exploration of dialogue
to carry on a story. Although the story is limited, her development as
a writer is evident in the way she uses conversation in her text. She
also demonstrated how she learned to use correct spelling and punctuation as she constructed her first drafts.

Word Study

In three classrooms, words were taught from a spelling book. All
children explored the same words. In the fourth classroom, children
were grouped for spelling based on the way they represented words.
In one group, children explored short-vowel words, and in another,
they explored long-vowel patterns.

Calvin, Bonnie, Fredy, and Julio were considered Letter-Name
spellers at the end of the year (Bear et al., 2004). They represented
single-syllable short-vowel words with an initial and final consonant

and a vowel, although the vowel might be confused. For example, they might spell *red* as RAD. They also used a vowel to represent a long-vowel pattern. For instance, they might write *tin* as TEN or *road* as ROD.

Anthony, Josie, Jaryd, Maria, Maritza, Heidee, Lucero, and Sandra were considered to be Within-Word-pattern spellers. They represented most single-syllable short-vowel words correctly. They struggled with representing long-vowel patterns; however, they no longer used a single vowel to represent the pattern. They might spell *road* as RODE or *cake* as CAEK.

One child, Eric, was considered a Syllable-Juncture speller, which meant that he could represent most single-syllable short- and long-vowel words correctly. He had difficulty knowing how to add an affix to a word. He puzzled about doubling or dropping letters. For example, he wrote *driving* as DRIVEING.

Summary of Second-Grade Literacy Learning

In second grade, students moved from simply decoding text to understanding it. They wrote about what they read and discussed books, both informational and narrative. They explored writing and learned about its conventions. They learned about words through spelling and moved beyond simple understandings about representing words to more complex ones in which two letters can represent a single sound.

The comments about learning to read in second grade are very different than the first-grade focus on words and decoding. For example, Anthony said, "I started liking reading this year." Lucero recounted, "I learned to write in second grade." And Eric thought that in second grade he "learned to read like a pro." These comments focus on motivation, the inclusion of writing, and becoming successful as a reader.

Third Grade

"Howie says he's bringing the whole family presents." She [Ramona] imagined bags of gold like those in *The Arabian Nights*, which Beezus had read to her.
—BEVERLY CLEARY (1984, p. 4)

Ramona connected experiences and words to those shared by authors, thus showcasing her knowledge of text and personal connections to it. In third grade, the students broadened their knowledge of books and became familiar with multiple texts and the connections across them.

In third grade, the children experienced having a single teacher in their classroom. No longer did they have teams of teachers for instruction. Their classrooms, while having fewer children than in rooms with two teachers, had more students that were the responsibility of a single teacher. Teachers utilized small-group and whole-group configurations. Most teachers had three ability groups for reading instruction. While the teacher met with each group, students were expected to be productively engaged with independent work and/or center activities.

Reading

Although teachers worked with students in reading groups, a major change during third grade was the amount of time that students read independently. Teachers had a wide range of reading material available to them, such as simple picture books, Accelerated Reader (AR) books (in which students took computerized quizzes to gain points), informational text, and numerous chapter books. For example, on one of my visits to a classroom, Lucero was reading an Arthur book—a picture book, Bonnie was reading an I Can Read book—a beginning chapter book, and Sandra was reading a *Little House on the Prairie* book—a novel.

As Sandra and a friend read a *Little House* book, I listened into their reading and conversation. Each child took turns orally reading, and the children freely corrected each other's miscues. After reading a page or two, they stopped and chatted. Sometimes to clarify a word meaning, such as *papoose*, they moved to Spanish and then made connections to what they thought the word meant in English. They hesitated when reading the word *molasses*, then Sandra said, "I like the sound of this word." I giggled with them when they broke out laughing as they read about long underwear. This conversation was typical of many that children had as they shared books they were reading in group or independently.

Students also wrote about their reading to develop comprehension. Most of their responses were summaries of text, rather than interpretive or personal responses. Maria's summary about *Cam Jansen and the Chocolate Fudge Mystery* (Adler, 1993) is representative.

> *Chapter 4—Cam's father was there with them. They picked up a newspaper and read it.* [no corrections]

These written responses were expected for books read in reading group but not for books read independently.

Several students changed their grade-level status during this year. Anthony joined the children considered to be above level in reading. He was the only student to elevate his status. Lucero and Maritza moved from above-grade-level readers to grade-level achievement. And Bonnie now was considered to be below grade level. Her teacher felt this was because "she spends more time talking than working."

During third grade, students encountered their first standardized achievement test—Terra Nova. None of the students scored at or above 50th percentile in the reading or vocabulary subtests. In reading, Eric, Sandra, Josie, Maria, and Lucero scored in the 40th percentile range, the highest scores for focal students. Heidee was the only child scoring in the 30th percentile in reading. Anthony and Fredy scored in the 20th percentile range. And Bonnie, Calvin, and Jaryd scored in the teens. Julio did not have sufficient English proficiency to take the test.

Vocabulary scores were interesting. In several cases, vocabulary scores were higher than reading scores, a surprising result with so many of these children learning English as a new language. Heidee, Jaryd, Calvin, and Lucero all scored higher in vocabulary than in reading.

Students were asked to write about the Terra Nova experience. Sandra wrote:

> *The Terra Nova test was kind of hard but not that hard because some questions were easy. I think it is important because teachers just check to see how you are doing. I studied so hard that my head hurt when I came home from school. I know that I am smarter because I studied.*

Students clearly knew that this test was important. Sandra thought it was so her teacher knew what she was doing in school. Other students worried that they might not move to fourth grade if they did not do well.

Writing

The biggest difference in third grade was writing. Children spent large periods of time writing in journals, and writing stories and reports.

In one classroom, students spent the first hour of each day writing in journals. On most days, they wrote to a teacher prompt. After students wrote, they shared their journals with other students. These students served as copyeditors for the writer. After copyediting, students could choose to read their entry with the class. Students were then expected to ask the writer about an interesting detail that he or she had not included.

One day, Anthony wrote about a buffalo picture that was tacked to the board.

> *This animal is a buffalo. It is a mammal. It has four legs. It's warm blooded. It has horns. It drinks from the pond. It has a lot of fur on its body. It is a big animal. It runs fast, very fast. It eats grass. [not corrected]*

When Anthony read this to the class, students wanted to know where buffaloes lived. He was not sure, so he went to the library at recess to find out on the Internet. He brought his answer back to class and shared it. This question generating and answering was common for these students as they learned to use resource materials to answer student-generated questions.

In other rooms, students spent time with a more traditional writing workshop. This was the year that students started to include their friends in their stories. For example, Lucero wrote:

> *Once upon a time there was a girl named Bonnie. Bonnie was wearing a blue shirt, blue shoes, and blue pants. Nobody ever*

> *saw her wear red or pink. Bonnie is eight years old. She was at school with Lucero, Gemessica, Jasmine, Maria, Michelle, and Tema. They were at their beautiful school and the name of the school was [Howard]. It has 200 classrooms, 200 bathrooms, and 200 teachers. Bonnie was the funniest person in the whole school. Their teachers were Mrs. Walker, Ms. Read, Mrs. Fryer, and Mrs. Erin. Bonnie always made everyone laugh in the middle of class and when she was always talking to Gemessica and Lucero, but when she got two alert slips she stopped talking to Lucero and Gemessica. Bonnie had to go to detention and Saturday school. She decided to stop talking in school.*

Although Lucero shared a vignette about Bonnie, her major goal was to get the names of her friends and teachers into this story. Her classmates loved hearing their names in print, although Bonnie reassured everyone that this story was not true.

Students also learned to write informational reports. All students were expected to write a report on an animal of their choice that included the following sections: cover, table of contents, name and description of animal, characteristics, defenses, food, habitat, effects of the animal, protection, illustrations, and bibliography. In May, each presented his or her report to the class. Each report was completed, with short paragraphs for each part. Eric wrote about boas and their food:

> *The boa eats monkeys, alligators, rabbits, deer and mice. It helps to keep less animals alive by eating them. If all these animals die the boa dies. If the boa dies there will be too many small animals. [no corrections]*

In addition to talking about the animals the boa eats, Eric allowed the reader to see the importance of a boa consuming so many small animals.

Word Study

Students engaged in daily word study. They built words using a Making Words strategy (Cunningham & Hall, 2003), or they sorted words. Once sorts were completed, students recorded them in word study notebooks.

In one example of word study, Bonnie found the following words that sounded the same but were spelled differently, with different meanings:

> *Knew—I knew a lot about frogs.*
> *New—I have a new car.*
> *Weak—Girls are weak. Not really.*
> *Week—There are seven days in a week.*

In other word studies, students found words that fit a particular pattern. Jaryd discovered that the following words had *oo* in them and sounded like the *oo* in *tooth—raccoon, boot, root,* and *balloon.*

Students' representations of words changed dramatically this year. Most children qualified as Syllable-Juncture spellers, who represented most single-syllable, short- and long-vowel words correctly. They struggled with adding affixes to words. Lucero moved to the most sophisticated level: Derivational Constancy. She understood how to add affixes and was exploring meaning elements in prefixes such as *dis, un,* and *mal.* And three students (Jaryd, Julio, and Calvin), still at Within-Word and exploring long-vowel patterns, were considered struggling readers and writers.

Summary of Third-Grade Literacy Learning

Students extended reading by participating in extended periods of silent reading. They frequently tested their reading comprehension with AR quizzes. They developed writing skills through daily writing experiences. They confidently wrote in journals, and wrote extended stories and reports. Word study was central to literacy instruction, and students focused on spelling and meaning of words.

Many of the students' comments about third grade included learning to read better and to read bigger books. The following are samples of their comments:

JOSIE: I learned how to read bigger, thicker books.

JARYD: I read big books.

JULIO: I read a lot of books.

ERIC: I read chapter books

FREDY: I learned about reading, because I love to read a lot.

Other students commented about writing:

SANDRA: I learned to write stories this year. I wrote about little girls and the wetlands.

HEIDEE: I like writing. I wrote a mammal report.

CALVIN: I wrote about my friends and kickball.

When reviewing their thoughts about third grade, students talked about specific stories and books they read. They shared favorite books and authors. They moved from generalities about reading and writing to specifics such as favorite stories they read or wrote.

Fourth Grade

Mrs. Whaley announced, "Today and from now on we are going to have Sustained Silent Reading every day." Ramona liked the sound of Sustained Silent Reading, even though she was not sure what it meant, because it sounded important.
—BEVERLY CLEARY (1981, p. 39)

Students in the fourth grade moved into three classrooms where, similar to Ramona, they spent a portion of each day involved in Sustained Silent Reading. Unlike Ramona, students were expected to take and do well on a quiz attached to each book. These quizzes indicated the book levels available to students for independent reading, and they determined grade-level achievement.

The teachers for the most part moved away from small-group literacy instruction; all students were engaged in the basal story and accompanying worksheets. In two classrooms, students participated in book club groups for a portion of the year. In book club groups students read novels orally to each other with limited discussion around the novel.

Reading

In two classrooms, students listened to their teachers read to them daily. Often students selected the text from a group of books, thus having a choice in this reading. Unfortunately, while their teachers were reading, few students listened in. For example, as the children listened to *Coming Home* (Hughes & Cooper, 1994), the teacher asked them about Langston Hughes. One child said that Hughes was black, and another said, "He wrote poetry." That was the end of conversation centered on reading. This example represented how only a small portion of students responded to this reading throughout the year. In many ways, the comments provided by students were similar to the single-word answers they offered in kindergarten.

Similar inattentiveness was apparent during whole-group basal reading. Teachers often explained the story extensively. I observed teachers asking students to predict what might happen and then answer the question themselves. Then students participated in vocabulary lessons in which new words and sentences were shared on an overhead transparency. Following is a brief example of this vocabulary work:

TEACHER: What is a mime?

STUDENT: A person who does not talk.

TEACHER: They pretend they are doing stuff—it is like a silent movie. A mime is an actor that never talks with words.

As seen in this example, one child answered, then the teacher elaborated on the definition. This conversation was teacher-directed, with few students paying attention. When students had to complete worksheets on this vocabulary, they were not aware of the meanings of the majority of words. They chatted with each other and guessed at what to write in the blanks. After the vocabulary work, students took turns orally reading the basal text. On subsequent days, students were expected to complete worksheets related to the text.

Students also engaged in the AR program for silent, independent reading. Many of the students discovered *Junie B. Jones* books, *Ramona* books, and other series during this year. In my field notes, I noted that there "was a wide range of books, from *Pokemon* to *Sounder*, in evidence as students independently read. Several students read from their own literature book, rather than choosing other literature. One student is reading Harry Potter." Students explored fiction during independent reading and found favorite authors and series; few students chose informational texts. When I asked students about their choices, they said, "Quizzes on information books are too hard."

At the end of the year, three students—Anthony, Eric, and Heidee—were considered to be above grade level. Eight students were at grade level—Bonnie, Calvin, Josie, Julio, Lucero, Maria, Maritza, and Sandra. And two students were below grade level— Fredy and Jaryd. This was the first year that Julio moved to grade-level achievement. During this year, Julio was placed on Ritalin and had a new stepfather, who was very interested in his learning. His stepfather stopped by school each day and made sure that Julio completed all unfinished work, both homework and assigned classwork. With this support, Julio's achievement was accelerated to meet grade-level expectations—a 2-year growth spurt during the year.

Students participated in standardized assessment and criterion-referenced assessment. I found that these test scores did not directly translate to standing in the class. Teachers relied on informal assessment and classwork to determine class placement, rather than these formal assessments. For instance, Josie scored 66% in reading and Maritza scored 60% in reading, and both were placed at grade level. Eric scored 58% and Heidee scored 51%, and both were considered above grade level.

The scores indicated that students did better on this assessment than on the one in third grade. Six children scored above the 50th percentile in reading; however, only one student (Eric) scored above the 50th percentile in vocabulary. Vocabulary scores were typically in the 20th percentile range. Jaryd and Bonnie scored the lowest in reading, with Jaryd also scoring the lowest in vocabulary.

For the criterion-referenced test (CRT), nine students scored above the 50th percentile; even Julio almost achieved this result with his 47th percentile in reading. Jaryd and Fredy had the lowest achievement on this test, with scores in the 30th percentile and 37th percentile, respectively.

What I found interesting during this year was that even though instruction did not appear to be engaging, and it was similar for all students, students achieved gains on these assessments. Perhaps, expecting all students to achieve at grade level, as demonstrated through the use of a single basal reader, made a difference. This was the first time that all students achieved the grade-level curriculum in reading. Or perhaps reading multiple books by the same author helped students develop reading skills.

Writing

Students frequently engaged in multiple forms of writing. They wrote in journals and wrote stories, reports, and letters. They also prepared for the state writing assessment by practicing different genres of writing, such as persuasive writing, and they learned about the traits of ideas, organization, voice, and conventions. Students participated in DOL activities that provided direct instruction and practice on spelling, grammar, and punctuation.

Teachers worked with students throughout the year, practicing for the big writing assessment. Students did get better at providing details, but they struggled with writing a cogent paragraph and focusing on the writing traits at the same time. In other writing, students produced lengthier text; they typically wrote one or two pages without much effort. They experimented with including voice in their writing and learned how to format paragraphs.

The following are two examples of the writing students did to practice for the state writing assessment; the first example is that of Bonnie, who scored low on the writing assessment:

> I felt scared and sad. I had no friends and I cryed a lot. I was really nervous the kids we're screaming. I was really shy but I got uste to it. It was always the same. But I didn't cry when I went to first grade or second grade now I'm a forth grader. I'm a big girl now I'm not a baby I was scared that the kids we're gonna hit me when I was in kindergarten. [no corrections]

The purpose of this practice assessment was to describe a first day of school. Bonnie's paragraph does not help us understand that she is writing about school until the end. She struggled with helping readers know the focus of her writing, providing sufficient detail, and using conventions.

The next example comes from Heidee, a student who scored high on this assessment, and wrote to the same prompt:

> *The first time at school was scary because I thought their were bullys and I thought I would not make friends but just then somebody came up to me and said do you want to play with me and I said yes to her except when I was in kindergarten people made fun of my name and called me names like Hidee-Hidee-Ho but only one person didn't make fun of my name and it was Tenika but everytime when she was there we have to be separated because we talk too much when were next to each other. So that is how I went through on my first day of school.*
>
> *But in first grade I made new friends and some old friends too except everytime my friends weren't there I would just sit near the wall or go to the swings and make other new friends. But every time their there I get pulled by one arm and get pulled by the other arm and every time they did that I just run-away or cry because they were doing that to me. So when it get to the third day I'd tell the princebal and that is how I went through when they did that and that is how I got new friends and old friends. Except that's why I didn't want to go to school on the first day. [no corrections]*

Heidee's paragraph, like Bonnie's, is missing important details and has problems with conventions. Heidee provides many details about friends but leaves out important information about what was happening on the playground. She also ends her writing by telling us that this is the reason she did not want to go to school, but framing this earlier would have made her writing stronger. The major differences between the pieces are length and organization; Heidee easily wrote a full page, with organized paragraphs, in the allotted time, whereas Bonnie struggled to complete one short paragraph.

For the state writing assessment, students were given a prompt and were scored with a rubric of 5 as the high score and 1 as the low score. Students received scores in four areas: ideas, organization, voice, and conventions. Bonnie and Jaryd had the most difficulty with this assessment, as reflected in their scores in the 1's and 1.5's. Josie, Lucero, and Heidee scored the highest, with 3's and 4's. Organization and conventions were areas in which students consistently scored the highest, reflecting the consistent, direct instruction provided by their teachers in these areas.

Word Study

For the most part, word study involved spelling words. In one classroom, the spelling list came from the basal reader. In the other classrooms, teachers used two or three lists. Students performed typical spelling activities such as writing their words multiple times and using them in sentences. On some occasions, they sorted words by pattern.

All of the students moved into the most sophisticated levels of word knowledge. Calvin, Jaryd, Julio, and Maritza were considered Syllable-Juncture spellers. They were learning about how to add affixes to words. All of the other students were Derivational-Constancy spellers. They were exploring the meaning elements of words. This development was quite sophisticated for fourth graders.

Summary of Fourth-Grade Literacy Learning

Reading instruction alternated between whole-group reading and independent reading. All students were expected to read the fourth-grade basal text. Writing instruction expanded beyond third grade in that students learned about different genres and how to write for a state assessment. Word study centered on spelling words that were not organized by any specific pattern. In one classroom words came from the basal text, and in the other classes they were developed by teachers. With this instruction, there were more students in the at-grade-level category. Only two students were considered to be struggling readers.

When I asked students about reading and writing during the fourth grade, the answer that came from them all was "I learned how to read chapter books." Josie, Sandra, and Anthony talked about reading at home as well. They were reading books like *Charlotte's Web* to their parents. A few students talked about writing, especially writing reports. Bonnie said, "I liked writing reports," and Anthony said, "I did book reports." They did not mention any of the other writing that occurred in their classrooms. And finally, when I asked them what was important about the fourth grade, they mentioned testing. They all knew that the tests were important to their teachers and parents.

Fifth Grade

There were words everyplace she looked: in books and newspapers, on signs and television, on cereal boxes and milk cartons. The world, Ramona decided, was full of people who used their dictionary skills and probably weren't any fun.
—BEVERLY CLEARY (1999, p. 108)

Fifth grade proved to be the year that students focused on words, the meanings of words as they appeared in the books the students were reading. Like Ramona, they learned to use dictionaries and thesauruses to improve vocabulary, spelling, and comprehension.

Students entered three fifth-grade classrooms; however, the teachers grouped students across classrooms for instruction. Each teacher took one reading group, with each group organized around below-, at-, and above-grade-level readers. Each teacher was also responsible for instructing all fifth-grade students in a content area such as math, social studies, and science. Students moved from room to room throughout the day for instruction. For reading, teachers used the basal text, novels, and AR for independent reading. Students had specific goals for AR, in which they had to read at a specified grade level, take quizzes, and secure good comprehension results.

Reading

Each day, students engaged in a 90-minute literacy block. The block always began with silent, sustained reading. In two classrooms, students worked alone as they read and took quizzes on their books. In the third classroom, the teacher conferred with students about their independent reading. If students wanted to read a book without an AR quiz, the teacher allowed them to develop a quiz. As I watched students during this time, I could always tell when they were pressed to reach an AR goal. Typically, students read chapter books that were worth more points in AR but took longer to read. When faced with a deadline, students chose picture books or simple chapter books, such as those in the *Frog and Toad* series, and quickly took as many quizzes as possible so that they reached their goal.

Following silent reading, students read their group novel and wrote about it. Each day, they took on a different expectation for writing, in which they might be a summarizer, a connector, an illustrator, or a vocabulary enricher. Often students quietly read next to each other and chatted about what they might write. Another group worked on spelling during this time, with the assistance of an instructional aide. And members of a final group discussed their book with the teacher. There was a rotation of groups, so that all groups participated in the three activities daily.

As students participated in reading instruction, they were very aware of their reading levels. They were guided in independent reading choices by the results of an AR placement test. Students were quick to tell me if they were at a 3.0 or a 4.5 level. And some students, such as Anthony and Eric, were displeased when they were not placed in the highest reading class. They concentrated on their reading and responses to reading, so that they were placed and stayed in the highest reading class. The status of being in "the best reading class" was very important to these boys.

Maria, Eric, Josie, Sandra, and Anthony were in the highest reading class, where they explored books from 4.5-5th grade reading levels. Maritza, Calvin, Julio, Bonnie, and Lucero were in the middle group, where they read books at the fourth-grade level. And Jaryd was in the lowest group, where he read books at the third-grade level.

As in previous years, teachers relied more on informal assessment to determine which students were at, above, or below grade level. Students took a CRT during fifth grade, in which scores ranged from a low of 30th percentile (Jaryd) to a high of 72.5th percentile (Anthony) in reading. While Anthony was considered above grade level and Jaryd below, other scores did not reflect students' grade-level placement. For example, Bonnie, with a 45th percentile, was at grade level, and Julio, with a 47.5th percentile, was below grade level.

Students also participated in AR assessment that resulted in a Lexile score that was converted to a grade-level range. Again, it was difficult to find consistency between the Lexile score and grade-level achievement. For example, Bonnie had a Lexile score of 874, which correlated to seventh grade, and Josie had a Lexile score of 892, which correlated to seventh grade, but Bonnie was considered at grade level and Josie above it.

Julio, Jaryd, and Calvin found themselves below grade level again. This was a consistent pattern since kindergarten, with a bit of fluctuation for each student to grade-level achievement. However, grade-level achievement proved difficult for them to hold on to; Julio even had the additional support of summer school and an after-school program to help him succeed. The majority of students maintained grade-level achievement—Bonnie, Eric, Josie, Lucero, Maria, and Maritza. This is an interesting result, because some of these students were in the above-grade-level reading block and others were in the grade-level block, thus demonstrating that the separation by ability did not result in students being at a particular level. And two students demonstrated above-grade-level achievement—Anthony and Sandra.

Writing

Teachers engaged students daily in the writing process through journals, responses to literature, and stories and reports. Teachers spent time helping students construct their pieces by focusing on revision and editing. Students also produced final drafts that they wrote using the computer. They became quite familiar with the computer helping them with spelling and grammar mistakes that they had overlooked. Lucero wondered, "Why didn't I know the computer could fix my mistakes?" They were enamored with the editing and spelling support available in their word-processing program.

One student, Maritza, became an engaged writer during this

year. She had a writing notebook and often stayed in during recess to write. She explored poetry writing consistently throughout fifth grade. One of her poems follows:

> I am a teacher
> I wonder if I will get to be a teacher
> I hear kids running to school
> I see kids studying
> I want to be a teacher
> I am a teacher
> I touch a desk and a pencil
> I work hard
> I am a teacher.

Teachers also used writing as a vehicle for reflection, so that students understood themselves as learners. For example, they wrote about themselves as readers. Maria wrote the following in her journal:

> When I started reading I was in kindergarten. I like it when something scary happened, or when something funny happened because I really get interested in it. I hate when I have to read in front of the class. I think it is fun but when I get up there I don't feel good because everybody's eyes are on me. You feel like you are being stared at. I feel like I am going to be sick. I hate to stand in front of the class. I would stay home if I could if I had to read in front of the class. [no corrections]

Many of the students wrote about liking to read but hating and being petrified of reading in front of the class. I wondered about this, because in fourth grade, all students were required to read orally to the class. They had conformed, but clearly this was not a practice they welcomed. They enjoyed silent reading and the conversations centered on reading that were common in fifth grade.

Word Study

Students pursued the meaning of words in fifth grade. They identified interesting or confusing words in their reading and then used resources such as dictionaries, glossaries, and thesauruses to discover their meanings. They recorded the words and their definitions in reading journals. For example, Lucero wrote:

Promoted. p. 33 to advance to the next higher grade. A verb.

When students reconvened in their reading groups, they discussed the words identified and their meanings. There was much conversation centered on the meaning of words.

Julio and Jaryd remained at Syllable Juncture throughout this year. Other students continued as Derivational-Constancy spellers and engaged in learning about the meaning of parts of words (affixes and bases) and whole words as shared in the example—*promoted.*

Summary of Fifth-Grade Literacy Learning

During fifth grade, silent reading and comprehension were valued by teachers and students. During reading group meetings, students engaged in discussion centered on meaning, and often on confusing words. Students wrote daily and became accustomed to serious revision and editing of their work. They learned how to support each other though revision and editing. And word study was centered on the meaning of words rather than just on the spelling of them.

When I chatted with students about reading and writing, they were very clear about how they knew whether they were a good reader or not. Most defined reading achievement through grades or AR goals. Calvin said, "I passed my goal in reading"; Maritza said, "I am not a good reader because I did not reach my goal"; and Anthony said, "I'm a good reader because I have lots of AR points." A few students noted new strategies they used to comprehend text. Maria said, "I visualize my reading this year," and Sandra noted, "I reread when I get confused. Sometimes the words are hard to figure out."

Students described themselves as writers as well. Calvin was displeased with his writing because he "used the same words over and over." Other students, such as Eric, Sandra, and Maritza, talked about the variety in their writing. They enjoyed writing poetry and plays.

This was the first year that students talked about their teachers. Calvin noted that "fifth grade is awesome because of my teachers." Julio said, "I like being with my teacher," and Sandra commented, "I like my teacher." During this year, all fifth-grade teachers opened their doors to students before and after school. Most students developed close friendships with their teachers, with whom they shared personal and academic concerns and successes.

Sixth Grade

She confiscated any notes written by her class that were sailed, passed, or dropped on desks. She then read them.
—BEVERLY CLEARY (1999, p. 105)

As I observed during sixth grade, I noticed students writing notes to each other and having private conversations whenever possible. Teachers spent amazing amounts of time collecting notes and chastising children for conversations during class time. However, students took risks and continued writing and chatting throughout the year. For many, friendships were more important than conforming to teacher expectations and often more important than academic reading and writing.

Students were placed into three sixth-grade classrooms. Two teachers shared students for instruction. One teacher taught all the students reading and writing in both classrooms. The other taught content areas of math and science. A third teacher taught her students herself and extended her school day by 15 minutes by deleting one recess. Afternoons were dedicated to reading and writing instruction, although teachers often had special classes like music or computers during this time.

Reading

In one classroom, students began the afternoon by reading AR books and taking quizzes. Then they listened to a story each day.

The teacher often spent extensive time discussing the plot or characters in the story. From this reading, students engaged in whole-group reading of their social studies text. They had packets of information and worksheets tied to the yearlong study of ancient cultures. Students also read novels that were connected to the social study theme. They met in small groups, where each student orally read from his or her novel. Students wrote summaries of their reading in a reading log.

Students in the other classes engaged in AR as well. From independent reading, they read in small groups throughout the classroom. The teacher moved from group to group and chatted with students about their reading. Students took turns orally reading their novels, then wrote about them in a journal. As students were engaged in reading, an instructional aide called groups to work with him on spelling. Content reading and writing occurred outside of the literacy block.

Although students were engaged in reading groups where they read novels, I found that most students only read two books during the year. Perhaps because they orally read to each other, the pacing was slow. Students read significantly more text during independent reading.

Soon after the beginning of the year, Julio left during the literacy block for small-group reading with a literacy specialist. Her goal was to get him to slow down and pay attention to comprehension. Because Julio loved to take AR quizzes and often failed them, he was made to write a summary of his story before he could take a quiz, and to read books at lower levels. Julio showed his frustration with this when he said, "This year, I got really low. I'm reading third-grade level. My teacher said I can't read sixth-grade level, so I'm not a good reader."

There was a huge shift in grade-level placement during sixth grade. The majority of students moved into the above-grade-level category. Two students remained at grade level. Unfortunately, Jaryd and Julio continued below grade level.

Students took a CRT in reading once again. Josie, Lucero, Anthony, Maria, Jaryd, Sandra, and Julio all did better in reading. There were no students scoring in the lowest quartiles on this test;

even Jaryd and Julio scored in the average range and met the school's expectations for annual yearly progress.

Students also participated in the AR assessment and had end-of-the-year Lexile scores. Maria, Anthony, and Sandra had Lexile scores that placed them at an eighth-grade independent reading level. Josie and Lucero were right at sixth-grade level for independent reading. While Eric and Maritza were considered to be above grade level in reading, their Lexile scores placed them at fifth-grade and fourth-grade levels, respectively. And Jaryd managed to achieve a fourth-grade level placement and Julio, a third-grade level. At the end of sixth grade, both boys were consistently demonstrating difficulty with reading, especially reading comprehension. Julio had additional reading help, but Jaryd was expected to learn to read with the regular curriculum in his classroom.

Writing

Students continued to write in journals, in response logs to reading and to content learning, and in stories and reports. They practiced for the state writing assessment. In the classroom where the teacher worked alone, she taught them a strategy for writing. For each piece they were to concentrate on a hook (the introduction), a line (the details), and a sinker (an important ending). For the other sixth-grade students, the focus was on the traits, and much of their writing was scored using the traits of ideas, conventions, organization, and voice.

For the state assessment, students wrote three-paragraph essays. For practice, teachers provided prompts similar to what might occur on the assessment. The following are two examples of the first paragraphs of these essays; the first, from Julio, is the first writing assessment in which he responded to the prompt of his house burning down:

> *Today I was really scared because my house was burning. I was saving my family. I was thinking the things I was saving. The first thing I was to save is my DVD with the movies. They were in my living room. That was when some of the fire from the roof fell in on my shoes. I took the DVD and the movies out-*

side. I would like to save my DVD because when we get another house we have a DVD. [no corrections]

Julio's writing starts with his family but quickly moves to his DVD. You can almost hear his teacher say, "Remember the details," as he adds why it is important to save his DVD. While Julio's writing can certainly improve, he wrote a paragraph that was cohesive, and he provided details.

Unlike Julio, Josie loved to write and wrote often in her notebooks both at school and at home. Her practice assessment was to write about a memory. The first paragraph of her writing follows:

Eight years ago I lived with my adoring father. The times we had together were fantastic. Well that is what my mom has been saying. My mom and my dad were divorced when I was three. She left and my dad cried so much. Nothing is left but a memory. My mom never talked about him (my dad). My mom says they never had a relationship. This is all I know, that his name is Jose and he was very wise. But me, I know nothing of the details of his dramatic life. [no corrections]

Josie writes with voice. She is aware of her audience and provides details so that her reader is not confused. She is also able to write a cohesive piece with mastery of the conventions.

Students' scores on the writing assessment improved. Jaryd experienced the most difficulty with this assessment, and it paralleled his difficulty with writing in the classroom. He avoided almost all writing assignments, unless he could write about wars and heroes. His scores showed that he needed support to develop as a writer. Julio took this assessment for the first time, and his scores were approaching the state expectation of 3. He managed to get a 3 on his writing sample in voice. The remaining students either scored 3's or 4's on the rubrics for each trait that met the state expectation.

Word Study

Word study instruction chiefly came from the books students read. They were expected to record difficult words and find their meanings. One teacher focused on vocabulary with students. Whenever she read to them, she highlighted interesting words. Students in the class tried to figure out their meanings and used dictionaries and thesauruses to help. For students in the other two sixth-grade classrooms, vocabulary was targeted through spelling lists. Students looked up words and used them in sentences.

I found it interesting that there was only one change in word knowledge as demonstrated in student writing. Anthony lost ground in that he moved from Derivational Constancy to Syllable Juncture. As Anthony wrote, he struggled with how to add affixes to words—knowledge he seemed to have had in previous grades. Perhaps during sixth grade, he was analyzing the shifts in words as affixes were added, and this additional concentration interfered with the automaticity he once displayed.

Summary of Sixth-Grade Literacy Learning

Sixth grade proved to be the year that students extended their knowledge and understandings of reading. Of the students I studied, only two were below grade level at the end of sixth grade. This important accomplishment is not usually expected in a high poverty school. Students also refined their writing skills and were able to write informally about their reading and learning, and formally through stories and reports. Word knowledge extended to include vocabulary related to math, social studies, and science.

Students understood that they had learned vocabulary and how to comprehend more difficult text. For instance, Josie said, "I learned more vocabulary words, and I read bigger books. And I could find the real meaning in it. More deeper—in poetry, because my teacher taught me how to find the meaning." Sandra, who was more specific about the kinds of words she learned, told me, "This year, I've learned new words and all verbs, pronouns, adjectives, and nouns, and all that. Yeah, I make my writing much more interesting too." Maritza also talked about meaning getting in reading when she said, "You understand what you're reading. 'Cause when I don't understand something, I go over it again." These comments demonstrate that students were very aware of the goals in teachers' instruction, and they appreciated their more sophisticated knowledge of reading and writing.

DISCOVERIES ABOUT LITERACY LEARNING

Variation in Grade-Level Achievement

The work of Juel (1994) and Stanovich (1986) highlights the importance of success in early literacy, because students who were behind in the primary grades stayed behind. My exploration sadly validates their research, in that Calvin, Julio, and Jaryd struggled with reading throughout elementary school. It is interesting that, of these three, only Julio came to school with a home language of Spanish. However, each of these boys did not always stay behind. They reached grade level (Calvin in first and fourth, Julio in fourth, and Jaryd in first); however, they were not able to retain this status for long. In most of their classroom experiences, they avoided or dawdled over reading and writing. In comparison to their peers, they read fewer books and almost no books at grade level, and they wrote shorter pieces of writing that rarely were revised. For these reasons alone, it was difficult for them to sustain grade-level achievement. Perhaps if they had been supplied additional literacy support daily, they would have been able to maintain grade-level expectations.

All three of these boys had Reading Recovery support in first grade; however, this support clearly was not sufficient. Julio also participated in afterschool and in-school literacy interventions. Again, this support was not enough. The only year in which Julio managed to attain grade-level status, fourth grade, was when he was on Ritalin and had support at home. It took medication and the support of his teacher, and particularly that of his parents, to gain this achievement.

I found it interesting that the school and teachers did not identify these boys for special assessment for special education support. Jaryd and Julio, in particular, were struggling readers. All assessments and school work supported this, but they were never recommended. Moreover, Julio, after brief Reading Recovery support in first grade, only received additional literacy support during school hours in the sixth grade, when he struggled with AR assessments and other schoolwork.

Although these boys followed the dismal predictions identified by Juel (1994) and Stanovich (1986), the other children did not. There was great variation in their achievement levels. For example, Sandra went from being a below-grade-level student in kindergarten and first grade to an above-grade-level student in succeeding grades. Anthony's grade-level status changed numerous times, at grade level in kindergarten, below it in first grade, at grade level in second grade, and above it in the remaining grades. As he moved into the intermediate grades, his status as a good reader was very important to him. Anthony often viewed reading skills and levels as a competition.

Phonemic awareness and phonics knowledge are known for their importance to reader success (Snow et al., 1998); however, in this study, they were not particularly predictive. A majority of students left kindergarten woefully lacking phonemic awareness, knowledge of letters, and understanding of sound–symbol relationships. They also struggled with understanding the language of instruction. By second grade, these students had developed alphabetic knowledge, they understood their teachers, and they were meeting grade-level and above-grade-level achievement in literacy. Perhaps the explicit focus on phonics and decoding in first grade was a necessary step in learning to read and write.

Additionally, a pattern in Table 2.2 demonstrates that a majority of students were below grade level in kindergarten. Then in second through fifth grade, the majority of students were in the at-grade-level category. A somewhat unexpected completion to this pattern is that in sixth grade, the majority were considered to be above grade level. These results are much more positive than might be expected for students in a high-poverty school. They document that teachers at all grade levels can make a difference in student achievement in reading. More importantly, they suggest that the dismal achievement statistics centered in high-poverty schools can be changed and are not as resistant as most teachers and the public believe.

Conforming to Expectations

As I observed students in a multitude of classrooms, I noted that students conformed to whatever teachers asked of them. In kindergarten, when the language of the teacher was very unfamiliar to them, they followed their teachers' pointing and the movement of other students, so that they did what the teacher expected, or what they thought the teacher expected. They learned to copy from one another and to color beautifully to please their teachers. And even though they were cramped together in a very small space for all learning activities, the children did not misbehave.

Students also adjusted to whole-class or small-group work in subsequent grades. If all students were expected to complete a similar assignment, they gave it their best effort. I never saw Jaryd or Julio complain that an assignment was too difficult, for instance. When students worked in small, ability groups, they conformed to working with the teacher and working independently. In all of my observations, they tried to meet the expectations of the teacher for behavior. The belief that students and classrooms would be disorderly or chaotic, and that learning would thus be sacrificed, was not true at Howard. And when a new principal came to the school, he quickly learned the name of each student, visited with them at recess, and let them know that this school was a safe school and he would not tolerate disrespectful behavior. His expectations were carried out by students, because they valued his friendship and leadership. They also appreciated being in a safe school, because their neighborhood was often threatening because of gang activity.

As students moved through the grades, this same, good student behavior stayed with them. Fourth grade was the only year when students such as Anthony balked at the teacher's expectations. He disliked his teacher and she disliked him. As a result, there were numerous power struggles throughout the year, with Anthony constantly being sent to the principal. It is interesting that while these power struggles were occurring, Anthony still achieved above grade level in reading.

The only other time that students were distracted from their teachers' expectations was in sixth grade, when students became very social and constantly passed notes among themselves. They also talked to their classmates after school and met at each other's homes. Note passing often became more important than the teachers' instruction; however, students still achieved at high levels. And they attempted to pass notes outside their teachers' observations, so that they were not directly disrupting instruction. There were great tensions between being a good friend and being a good student during sixth grade.

Support for ELLs and Struggling Readers

Students at Howard, no matter what their home language, were expected to achieve in literacy at the same time, and with the same benchmarks, as their peers. There was no additional time or accommodations for children whose home language was not English to accomplish learning expectations. And all instruction was in English.

In some classrooms, instructional aides worked with students, especially those who had difficulty with classroom assignments. In second grade, the instructional aides enhanced instruction. They worked with small groups of students on Readers' Theatre productions, for instance. Students practiced with the instructional aide and performed for classmates. In other grades, for the most part, instructional aides helped students with questions about independent work and corrected work.

In one kindergarten and one second-grade classroom, teachers helped students make connections between home language and school language. Children in one kindergarten classroom helped their teacher learn Spanish words. She often asked students to provide a word in Spanish for one she was teaching in English. Students loved helping her and playing the part of a teacher. In second grade, one of the teachers learned English as a new language. She frequently praised her students' mastery of English. When a student like Julio struggled to find the right word, she recommended that he talk to other students in Spanish for help. It was not uncommon to see Julio talking to his teacher, leaving to query another student about a word, and then returning to continue his conversation with the correct word in place.

Although students accomplished quite well in reading and writing, they often commented on the difficulty of vocabulary. Josie and Sandra both frequently mentioned that it was the words that made reading hard. For example, Sandra said, "I have to reread, because I don't know what all the words mean. I look them up, but I am not always sure that I know them." This is not surprising, because these students learned to read and write while they learned English. Whereas vocabulary was not a huge issue for comprehension in the primary grades, it became a central issue for comprehension in the intermediate grades, where vocabulary was more abstract in meaning and more central to content understanding. This difficulty with vo-cabulary was evidenced in students' vocabulary scores on standard-ized assessment measures.

In addition to ELLs, other students also experienced difficulty in learning to read and write. Reading Recovery was available to selected students in first grade. Although Reading Recovery helped students such as Bonnie, Maritza, and Sandra become successful in literacy, students such as Jaryd and Julio needed more. Unfortu-nately, they did not receive systematic, additional support to meet grade-level expectations. Julio participated in after-school reading, summer school, and a pull-out program in the sixth grade. However, he needed more systematic support throughout the grades, not just when he was in fifth and sixth grades.

Howard Elementary was aware of these problems with support-ing ELLs and struggling readers. They implemented additional sup-port for struggling readers through literacy specialists who worked with students at each grade level. Unfortunately, this support was put in place too late to help the students whose progress I followed. In addition to literacy specialists, teachers at Howard participated in professional development that targeted the needs of ELLs. The ex-pectation was that each teacher would better be able to enhance the learning of ELLs. They recognized the need to focus on vocabulary for all students.

The good news about literacy learning is that these students were successful with minimal support for their ELL needs. They managed to meet grade-level and above-grade-level expectations in literacy in a new language. Their early difficulties with learning the code were not predictive of future achievement. However, what might their literacy achievement have been had they had systematic support in learning English or with their struggles in learning to read and write? This is a question I continued to ponder at the conclusion of this exploration.

REFERENCES

Adler, D. (1993). *Cam Jansen and the chocolate fudge mystery.* New York: Puffin Books.

Bear, D., Invernizzi, M., Templeton, S., & Johnston, F. (2004). *Words their* way: Word study for phonics, vocabulary, and spelling instruction (3rd ed.). Upper Saddle River, NJ: Prentice-Hall.

Bruner, J. (1999). *The culture of education.* Cambridge, MA: Harvard University Press.

Cleary, B. (1968). *Ramona the pest.* New York: Avon Books.

Cleary, B. (1975). *Ramona the brave.* New York: Avon Books.

Cleary, B. (1977). *Ramona and her father.* New York: HarperTrophy.

Cleary, B. (1981). *Ramona Quimby, age 8.* New York: HarperCollins.

Cleary, B. (1984). *Ramona forever.* New York: Avon Books.

Cleary, B. (1999). *Ramona's world.* New York: Morrow.

Cole, M., & Wertsch, J. (1996). Beyond the individual–social antinomy in discussions of Piaget and Vygotsky. *Human Development, 39,* 250–256.

Cunningham, P., & Hall, D. (2003). *Hands-on developmentally appropriate spelling and phonics activities.* Redding, CA: Good Apple Publications.

Dubowski, C. (1987). *Pretty good magic.* New York: Random House.

Gee, J. (1985). The narrativization of experiences in the oral style. *Journal of Education, 167,* 9–35.

Gee, J. (1990). *Social linguistics and literacies: Ideology in discourses.* London: Falmer Press.

Gee, J. (2002). *Social linguistics and literacies: Ideology in discourses* (2nd ed.). Bristol, PA: Taylor & Francis.

Hughes, L., & Cooper, F. (1994). *Coming home.* New York: Putnam.

Juel, C. (1994). *Learning to read and write in one elementary school.* New York: Springer-Verlag.

Marshall, H. (1992). Seeing, redefining, and supporting student learning. In H. Marshall (Ed.), *Redefining student learning: Roots of educational change* (pp. 1–32). Norwood, NJ: Ablex.

Martin, R., & Shannon, D. (1992). *The rough-face girl.* New York: Putnam.

National Reading Panel. (2000). *Teaching children to read: An evidence-based assessment of the scientific research literature on reading and its implications for reading instruction: Reports of the subgroups.* Washington, DC: National Institute of Child Health and Human Development.

Numeroff, L. (1985). *If you give a mouse a cookie.* New York: HarperCollins.

Ramirez, J., Yuen, S., Ramey, D., Pasta, D. (1991). *Final report: Longitudinal study of structured English immersion strategy, early-exit, and late-exit transitional bilingual education program for language minority children.* San Mateo, CA: Aguirre International.

Snow, C., Burns, M., & Griffin, P. (1998). *Preventing reading difficulties in young children.* Washington, DC: National Academy Press.

Stanovich, K. (1986). Matthew effects in reading: Some consequences of individual differences in the acquisition of literacy. *Reading Research Quarterly, 21*, 360–406.

Sulzby, E. (1985). Children's emergent reading of favorite storybooks: A developmental study. *Reading Research Quarterly, 20*, 458–481.

Yopp, H.K., & Yopp, R.H. (2000). Supporting phonemic awareness development in the classroom. *Reading Teacher, 54*, 130–143.

Chapter 3

Learning from Teachers

[Teachers] mediate children's activity and experience, and help them make sense of learning, literacy, life, and themselves.

—PETER H. JOHNSTON (2004, p. 2)

Johnston's words echo the importance of teachers to student development, both academic and personal. Numerous writers and researchers have documented teachers as the single most important component to student success (Barone, 2003; Block & Mangieri, 2003; Ladson-Billings, 1994; Waxman, Padrón, & Gray, 2004). Teachers at high-poverty schools in particular understand that the demographics shared by students do not define them or limit their life possibilities. Student learning happens because of the informed decisions that teachers make about selecting appropriate materials and strategies to nurture student development (Mazzoni & Gambrell, 2003). Teachers at a high-poverty school like Howard are especially critical to academic success as they nudge students from their current literacy understandings to those valued by the middle class and, for many students whose home language is not English, to conversational and academic English. Although many students at this school read and wrote at home with parents and siblings, they relied on Howard's teachers for an understanding of mainstream ways and expectations for reading and writing.

Teachers at Howard participated in ongoing professional devel-

opment centered on literacy. They utilized a professional development model called Comprehensive Early Literacy Learning/Extended
Literacy Learning (CELL/ExLL; for more details about this model,
visit www.cell-exll.com). Within this model, teachers explored articles about exemplary literacy practices, discussed them, and brought
these practices to their students. They had a primary and intermediate literacy specialist available to help with in-class instruction. This
ongoing professional development was consistent through all my
years of observation, although it infrequently targeted students of
poverty or ELLs. In addition to this professional development focused on literacy, various teachers engaged in other professional development activities that targeted the needs of ELLs, mathematics,
and other topics. Many of the teachers also participated in National
Board certification activities. At present, six teachers have achieved
this status.

    In the previous chapter, I presented a grade-by-grade overview of
student learning. In this chapter, rather than providing such a linear
perspective, I share background about teachers' professional experience, then take a more global look at literacy instruction across the
grades. From this broad background, I share some of the teachers'
exemplary and not so exemplary literacy practices as they taught
their students to read and write. I also look at exemplary practices to
support ELLs. These vignettes facilitate a deeper understanding of
the instruction provided to students at Howard.

TEACHERS AT HOWARD ELEMENTARY

The teachers at Howard had a great range in experience (see Table
3.1 for specific details about teachers). Of the 29 teachers who had
focal students, two were in their first year of teaching. Mrs. Stew-
art, a second-grade teacher, and Mrs. Fryer, a third-grade teacher,
were new to teaching the year that I observed. The majority of
teachers (20) had from 2 to 7 years of experience. Six teachers had
from 11 to 20 years of experience. Many of the teachers had been
at Howard for several years. During my study, there was teacher
turnover, but the percentage of teachers each year who chose to

TABLE. 3.1. Overview of Teacher Experience and Issues

Grade level	Teachers		Issues
Kindergarten	Mrs. Harter	Mrs. Martin	Not enough time.
	15 years: 1 year in K, special education	11 years: 2 years in K, 1, 2, 3, 4, 5	Teachers should be here for the kids.
			Kids are so far behind.
	Mrs. George		
	3 years: 2 years in special education, conduct-disordered class		
First grade	Mrs. Kirby & Ms. Mears	Mrs. Cullen & Mrs. Adams	Better understanding of expectations with professional development.
	Kirby—4 years: 3 years in 1–2; 1 year in 1, 2, 3	Cullen—5 years in 1	Team teaching is hard.
	Mears—2 years: 1 year in 1; 1 year in 1–2	Adams—6 years: 2 years in 4; 9 years as sub; 2 years in art; 2 years in 1	A good year and kids progressed.
	Mr. Shott & Mrs. Sims	Mrs. Messina & Mrs. Denton	Need more leveled readers.
	Shott—30 years in broadcasting; 7 years in teaching: 1 year in 3; 3 years in 2; 2 years in 1–2; 1 year in 1	Messina—15 years in 1; fluent in Spanish	Kids going to Mexico is a problem.
	Sims—7 years: 3 years in 3 and 4; 2 years in 3; 2 years in 1	Denton—7 years in 1; 2 years in 4 and 5	Variety of levels within basal stories is hard to deal with.
			Vocabulary not familiar to students.
			Discipline needed at school.
			Losing good teachers.

(continued)

TABLE. 3.1. (*continued*)

Grade level	Teachers				Issues
Second grade	Mrs. Stewart & Mrs. Harrison	Mrs. Scott & Mrs. Ford	Mrs. Stevens & Mrs. Smith		After-school program is helpful.
	Stewart—first year Harrison—20 years in special education; 1 year in 2	Scott—1 year in 4 Ford—5 years: 4 years in 4; 1 year in 1	Stevens—2 years in 2; National Board teacher; learned English as a new language Smith—2 years in 2; National Board teacher		Fewer children in lowest quartile; 3-year trend.
					Four Reading Recovery teachers made a difference.
					Two facilitators helped teachers.
					We are tired, the room being painted in the middle of the year, mapping curriculum, professional development, after-school programs.
					Each teacher able to buy $1,200 worth of books.
					No support for kids struggling in reading in second grade.
Third grade	Mrs. Walker	Ms. Read	Mrs. Fryer	Mrs. Erin	Hardest year so far.
	6 years in 1, 2, 3; National Board teacher	7 years in 1 and 4	First year	4 years in 1–2 and 3	The kids couldn't comprehend what they read.
					I am going to first grade, where the kids won't be behind.
					I loved it. It was a dream come true.
					I worked hard this year and I was disappointed with the scores on the Terra Nova.

Fourth grade	Mrs. Chew	Mrs. Spears	Mrs. Scott	
	2 years in K, 4	4 years: 2 years in 2; 1 year in K; 1 year in 4; owned preschool	2 years in 4	Loved class, hard-working kids.
				A growing period. I hate spending time teaching to the test. We did a reading comprehension packet to prepare.
				Wonderful year as far as the children are concerned.
				Big problem is comprehension. They read but don't understand.
				I dream of what it would be like to teach in a different school.
Fifth grade	Mr. Bussoni	Mrs. Katen	Mrs. Callep	
	17 years: 9 years in 5; 8 years combined in 1 and 2	2 years in 5	6 years: 3 years in 4 1 year in K–1; 2 years in 5	A dynamic year. We piloted the fifth-grade organization where we share the kids in all subjects. The high group [in reading] moved way beyond where they normally are—a higher level of thinking. The grouping helped us focus on individuals.

(continued)

TABLE. 3.1. (continued)

Grade level	Teachers			Issues
	Mr. McGuire	Ms. Jones	Ms. Booth	
Sixth grade	2 years in 6	14 years in 6; National Board teacher	20 years as preschool counselor; 6 years in 1, 2, 3, 5, 6; waiting to hear about National Board results	Kids got along; they understand each other. When a child is having a bad day, other kids move in to help.
				These kids have a lot of resilience, you know, perseverance. They have an I-can-do-it attitude.
				This was a smooth year. They are engaged in reading and writing. They are the highest-scoring class on the writing assessment I have ever had.
				The kids were motivated to read. They were easy to teach. I tried book clubs.

leave was small. At first, teachers who left said it was because of the morale at the school. However, when a new principal came on board, most teachers left because they were moving to another state. This stability is unusual, because at most high-poverty schools, many teachers do not even survive until the end of their first year (Brown, 2002).

The final column in Table 3.1 highlights issues that teachers shared during end-of-the-year interviews. Kindergarten teachers were most concerned with the shortness of their academic day (only 3 hours and no class on Friday because of professional development) and their students' struggle with the curriculum. Interestingly, they did not mention any difficulties that were manifested because the majority of their students were ELLs. First-grade teachers found that teaming with another teacher was difficult. First- and second-grade teachers team-taught because of the class size reduction in place but this left insufficient stand-alone classrooms for each teacher. It took extra time to plan together as a team, and they did not always agree on curricular or classroom management issues. In fact, in one first grade, teachers taught in the same room, but only one teacher taught at a time. Often the other teacher left the room while her partner taught. First-grade teachers also acknowledged the benefit of on-site professional development.

Second-grade teachers had positive attitudes and valued the interventions that were available to first-grade students. They noted that Reading Recovery helped students attain grade-level expectations. Unlike the second-grade teachers, third-grade teachers were discouraged. They did not feel that their students comprehended well, and they were disappointed that their efforts did not result in greater student learning as measured on achievement tests. Unfortunately, they were not sure why these results happened; therefore, they were not focused on implementing specific strategies to change this result. Fourth-grade teachers also noted that students struggled with comprehension. One teacher commented that she wanted to go to a school where "parents supported students more and where students were not poor." This teacher let student demographics block her teaching and personal relationships with students. Brown (2002) documented that some teachers in high-poverty schools seek to teach in other schools, where they think teaching will be easier because of student demographics.

Fifth- and sixth-grade teachers were optimistic and did not really highlight issues. They were pleased with student learning and the way students handled themselves. They recognized that students did well on tests and were very motivated to read and write. Importantly, fifth- and sixth-grade teachers, with the exception of one sixth-grade teacher, worked with all students at a grade level. They talked about all of the students within a grade rather than just their own classrooms. These teachers created broad grade-level communities rather than isolated communities of students within a single classroom. As a result, teachers collaborated about how to support individual students and found time to build personal relationships with them.

When thinking about the issues noted by teachers, I found it interesting that they varied so much. For the most part, few new students entered these rooms over the years. Although students were rearranged within classrooms each year, the makeup of students across each grade was similar. However, teachers viewed students very differently, seeing them either as struggling or as successful students from year to year. These perspectives were very important to student achievement regardless of the academic strengths or needs that students brought with them as they entered a new grade.

LITERACY INSTRUCTION
IN THE PRIMARY GRADES

Kindergarten

I separated kindergarten from the other primary grades because instruction was so different and unique to kindergarten. Kindergarten teachers chose to teach all of their students in whole-group instruction (Barone, 2002a). In Mrs. Harter's room, students began most days looking at books and then listening to a story or engaging in a phonics-based activity. Once this was concluded, students moved to tables, where they copied words and pictures into a journal, completed a math sheet, or worked on other independent activities. Because the space in kindergarten rooms was so cramped, students did not have center activities with freedom of movement. All independent activities were situated at tables.

Mrs. Harter envisioned her students engaged in rich conversations about the books she selected for them to read. At the beginning of the year, she often stopped and encouraged students to discuss the text she had just read. However, because most of her students were learning English, they did not possess the oral language strengths in English to discuss books. They might say, "Sad," "Happy," or "Mad," but Mrs. Harter had visions of deep conversations, not single-word responses. Because of students' struggle with conversation, these times were shortened and eventually became nonexistent as the year progressed. Meier (2003) indicated that Mrs. Harter's experiences were not unique. ELLs often are not familiar with narrative text, do not know how to answer questions that have obvious answers, or have sufficient English vocabulary to participate. Not surprising was Mrs. Harter's frustration with this result, but she did not have the skills to scaffold her students' current proficiency with English and encourage discussion as students became more proficient in their oral interactions with books.

Mrs. Harter constantly tried new strategies with her students. For example, in the middle of the year, she had students choose words that were personally meaningful to them, write them on cards, and learn to read and write them. Although students enjoyed this activity and were developing a rich collection of words they could read and write, the classroom management issues of working with only one student at a time ended this activity. She said, "I know this works. I see them learning words. I just can't do it alone." I found it interesting that she did not see her instructional aide as being able to help with this personalized instruction.

In the other kindergarten class, two teachers shared a contract and taught on different days. When Mrs. George taught, students informally chatted with her for an hour each day. She often asked students to teach her Spanish words, and they explored similarities and differences between Spanish and English words. She also had each child spell his or her name each day. From these discussions, students moved to tables, where they completed worksheets independently.

On days when Mrs. Martin taught, she read a big book to students, then they chorally read it. Following reading, students moved to tables, where they might hear another book with a follow-up activity or complete worksheets. Mrs. Martin worked at one table, and she secured older students to work at other tables.

When I look back at kindergarten classes, several observations are noteworthy:

1. Teachers taught to the whole class, not to individual students. All students were expected to complete the same assignments regardless of home language. All assignments were completed in class. Teachers only sent work or books home that were completed or read in class.
2. Students had minimal opportunities to engage with text. They never explored leveled text even though it was available in the school.
3. Instruction focused on letter recognition and sound–symbol relationships.
4. All student work was expected to be correct. Most writing involved copying.
5. Professional development that only targeted literacy strategies, without combining them with ELL issues, was not successful. Teachers quickly abandoned new strategies, for either they did not appear successful with ELLs or teachers did not believe they had the necessary support.
6. Teachers did not include parents in instruction; the only communication with parents was in conferences.

I left kindergarten reflecting on the first experiences of school for the majority of these children. They learned to follow directions, but most instruction was not meaningful. There was little conversation between teachers and students. Perhaps most discouraging was the minimal support for ELLs. Mrs. George was the only kindergarten teacher who orally explored words in English and Spanish with her students. ELLs were just expected to understand all the curriculum, with few, if any, real accommodations. When I compared these teachers to those described by Block and Mangieri (2003), they could not be considered as *guardians*.

Kindergarten teachers at Howard focused on the alphabet and sound–symbol instruction for all students. They expected students' work to be correct and did not provide opportunities to explore reading and writing in ways that nurtured students' early attempts at reading and writing. Their curricular agenda was clear, and they consistently pursued it: kindergarten students must know the alphabet and sound–symbol relationships to be successful in later grades. Unfortunately, the majority of students left with minimal knowledge about the alphabet even after daily, systematic exploration of it. Even more important to future success, students left without creating personal relationships with their teachers, and their parents were not encouraged to become involved in their academic learning.

First, Second, and Third Grades

Teachers in the primary grades provided quite similar literacy instruction. They broke students into groups based on current literacy knowledge that was informed through informal assessment, most often running records. During the first weeks of school, teachers asked students to write for 10 minutes, to list all the words they knew, to complete a developmental spelling list, and to participate in running records. They used this information to form groups for directed instruction in reading. In classes with teams of teachers, there were typically six ability-based groups. In third grade, where there was a single teacher, students were placed into three ability-based groups. Each day students worked with their teacher on guided reading, then completed independent work and went to centers.

Only one first-grade team varied from this structure. Mrs. Cullen and Mrs. Adams organized literacy instruction by having students copy several sentences from the board. These sentences usually related to the day. For example, students might copy, "Today is Thursday. It is raining. We have to stay in for recess." Following copying, students moved to the library, where they freely chose reading material for the next hour. Unfortunately, most of the books were too difficult for these students to read. They were picture books with difficult vocabulary and no predictable or decodable patterns. To conclude the literacy block, teachers broke students into two groups.

Each teacher took one group and read the children a story from the basal text. Students then completed worksheets related to the selection from the basal text. Students were not expected to read these text selections independently.

Although there was variation in the way teachers crafted their day, for the most part, the following activities occurred daily in all but one first-grade classroom:

- Independent reading
- A word wall with activities to develop sight word knowledge and to support spelling
- Journal writing, most often with a teacher-directed topic
- Phonics and spelling instruction
- Directed oral language activities (students corrected sentences with errors)
- Guided reading groups using basal and leveled text
- Shared reading
- Read-alouds

In second and third grade, the following practices were added:

- Comprehension of informational and narrative texts
- Writing workshop

First-grade teachers focused for the most part on decoding skills. Their major emphasis was on getting students to decode text easily. When working with small groups of students, they listened in as students orally read, and they helped with difficult words. In second and third grade, there was a huge shift in instruction toward comprehension. Teachers spent considerable time having students predict what might happen when reading a narrative selection or in creating charts to help with comprehension of informational text.

When comparing these teachers to other teachers documented in the research, first-grade teachers certainly realized the need to have students develop phonemic awareness and phonics knowledge (National Reading Panel, 2000; Yopp & Yopp, 2000). Unlike the teachers that Block and Mangieri described (2003), they did not engage in complex instruction. They simplified literacy instruction by focusing on sound–symbol relationships (Barone, 2002b).

Second- and third-grade teachers built on the decoding knowledge that students brought to second grade. As seen in Table 3.1, they valued students' ability to decode text and thought that classroom instruction plus Reading Recovery support was responsible. Their task, as they saw it, was to help students advance from just reading the words to comprehending what was read. They extended the content of student reading by systematically bringing in informational text. Moreover, they expected students to write in journals, to write about their reading, and to write stories and reports. These teachers matched the exemplary teachers described by Block and Mangieri (2003) in that they used multilevel material to meet current student knowledge, and they scaffolded ways for students to gain understanding of text. They also understood the importance of small-group work in developing student comprehension (Taylor, Pearson, Clark, & Walpole, 1999).

As I observed second- and third-grade teachers, I realized that they were using their entire day to build literacy knowledge and understanding. Social studies and science were carefully taught through reading. For instance, experiments in science followed or extended reading content. Ms. Read shared her thoughts about how the curricular focus changed:

> "They were not readers. Many of them were decoders, but not real readers. No comprehension about what they were reading; can't infer; they're not getting information from what they are reading. That bothered me. So I brought in things like tadpoles and took them on field trips. We went everywhere to farms, ballets, hikes, parks, you name it. Now they write better and they understand what they read. They are excited to write about our trips and what they learned. We study oceans and farms, and things like that so I can connect what we see to what they read. I know they are seeing the connections now."

Ms. Read was not alone. Rather than just focus on reading and writing in the classroom, teachers broadened the walls of their classrooms to include the community surrounding the school. Students frequently went on field trips to see firsthand topics of study. These trips certainly supported literacy learning of ELLs. In this way, teachers provided critical experiences for students, then connected them to in-class reading, writing, and learning.

Second- and third-grade teachers abandoned any preconceived notions about maintaining low expectations for students; they found ways to build on student strengths and extend their understanding (Reglin, 1995). For instance, when students did not comprehend, they used graphic organizers, discussion, and field trips to build comprehension. They also used language, both oral and written, as a tool for deeper understanding (Gutierrez, Basquedano-Lopez, & Turner, 1997). They were persistent and determined that their students would be academically successful. They took responsibility for this expectation.

LITERACY INSTRUCTION
IN THE INTERMEDIATE GRADES

Fourth Grade

It may appear strange to single out fourth grade; however, the instruction in fourth grade was very different from that provided in first through third and in fifth and sixth grades. Therefore, to understand this critical year in the literacy development of students, I have separated it from the others.

There were three fourth-grade classrooms at Howard. Each of the teachers relied on whole-class literacy instruction. The upside of this instruction was that all students engaged in shared literacy practices and discussions. The downside was that there were no direct attempts to meet individual student needs (Reutzel, 2003). All students engaged in the same selection from the basal text, then completed worksheets related to the selection. Often students took turns reading parts of the selection orally to the class in a round-robin fashion. For the most part, vocabulary related to basal text selections was taught through the use of overheads. A brief excerpt of a vocabulary lesson that related to a story about a circus in the basal follows:

TEACHER: What is a *vagabond*? This is a person who travels from place to place. They go somewhere new each day.

[Students read the sentence with vagabond.]

TEACHER: What is *retired*?

STUDENT: When you quit something.

TEACHER: Yes old people usually retire. They live on the money they have saved. These are the golden years.

[Students read the sentence with retired.]

TEACHER: What is *trance*?

The teacher moved through the list of words this way before students explored the story. When I reviewed numerous lessons on vocabulary, I found that teachers did most of the talking and students provided brief definitions. And if students did not know the meaning of the word, teachers explained, as seen with the word *vagabond*. Practice of this vocabulary occurred when students completed worksheets.

Later in the year, two teachers added reading groups in which students read the same novel. The literacy specialist worked with teachers to extend their literacy curriculum beyond such a narrow focus on the basal text. However, as teachers began these groups, they asked students to read the novel orally to one another, with little to no time for discussion. The fourth-grade teachers were not comfortable working with small groups as the year ended. In fact, even when students read in small groups, they all did so together, with the teacher moving from group to group.

Students also had time each day for independent reading. Students chose Accelerated Reader (AR) books, then took quizzes on them.

All students participated in daily oral language (DOL), where they were expected to write the convention corrections for each sentence. They also wrote in journals and completed stories and reports. Most writing was in preparation for the state writing assessment, although students wrote book- and content-oriented reports too.

The only variation I saw in curriculum was in spelling. In one class, students learned spelling by studying the words provided in the basal text. In another classroom, the teacher selected words for students to learn. In yet another class, there were three spelling groups based on students' word knowledge (see Bear, Invernizzi, Templeton, & Johnston, 2004).

A comparison of fourth-grade teachers and the exemplary teachers described by Block and Mangieri (2003) revealed that the former were more directors than coaches. Instruction for the most part was explicit and to the whole class, followed by independent practice. However, whereas Mrs. Chew and Mrs. Scott remained distant from their students and did not build personal relationships, Mrs. Spears did. She found time each day to quietly talk to each student either about something that happened at home or something she noticed in school. One day, I heard her tell Calvin, "I noticed that you did all of your work and I can see your motivation." These private comments motivated students to challenge themselves and deepen their literacy knowledge.

Unlike second- and third-grade teachers, two fourth-grade teachers were not consistent in their optimism about students or in their ingenuity to support student learning. Mrs. Chew, for instance, often talked about the struggles her students had with writing. A couple of her comments follow:

> "I taught my students how to do a five-paragraph book report this year. They really had a hard time."
> "I can't make them do a huge report because these kids can't handle huge reports."

Mrs. Chew struggled with what she observed as her students' accomplishments and puzzled about how "these kids" could do better. She believed that their home circumstances limited their in-school achievement. Whereas Mrs. Chew found her students to be lacking in knowledge, Mrs. Spears described her students as competent and exciting. A few of her comments follow:

> "I kept telling them that they are smart, really smart. Now they want to accomplish more. They want to go to college."
> "I love when they write. They connect personal things. I love

their honesty. It's just the tender things they write that get to
me."

"They can comprehend what they are reading."

While there were many contributing factors in end-of-grade-
level achievement and assessment, students in Mrs. Spears's classroom scored the highest on the Terra Nova and the state writing
assessment. Students in Mrs. Chew's class struggled with the state
writing assessment; Sandra and Maria did the best, with an average
of 2.5. As I observed in these rooms throughout the year, it was
evident that Mrs. Chew only saw the things her students could not
do or their struggles with learning. Mrs. Scott also decided early in
the year that her students had many learning difficulties, and she
spent the majority of her year planning on leaving Howard. Unlike
her two grade-level colleagues, Mrs. Spears chose to work persis-
tently with her students' current strengths and nudge them toward
more ambitious goals for learning then and in the future. Importantly, although classroom instruction was similar, the personal
connections shared in Mrs. Spears's classroom contributed to student learning.

Fifth and Sixth Grades

There were three fifth-and sixth-grade classrooms. In fifth grade,
teachers organized instruction across the grade. These teachers informally assessed their students in literacy and math. All teachers
worked with students on literacy, with students regrouped based on
current literacy or math knowledge. Each teacher kept his or her
homeroom for AR practice. For content areas, one teacher taught
math, another taught science, and the third, social studies. When the
teachers presented this plan to the principal, he was skeptical. He
worried that students would spend most of the day moving from
class to class. In response, teachers guaranteed that transitions would
be speedy and efficient. Their planning facilitated smooth transitions
that occurred in less than 2 minutes. Students knew the routines and
the academic and behavioral expectations of all of their teachers, because they were consistent among the rooms. All teachers used a

token economic strategy for classroom management, in which one student jotted down the names of students behaving appropriately, and students earned money that could be spent on small items (classroom supplies) or large items with money accumulated throughout the year (a computer).

In sixth grade, two teachers continued with the instructional organization created in fifth grade. They organized differently, in that one teacher taught literacy and the other, math. Students were placed into two groups. Each teacher kept his or her homeroom students for AR practice, although students picked books from either classroom. One teacher taught science and the other, social studies. Because the classrooms shared a common door, transitions were again efficient. One teacher, Ms. Booth, worked alone; she chose not to participate in shared teaching with the other sixth-grade teachers. She also extended her school day by eliminating an afternoon recess for her students. Her literacy block stretched from 12:15 to 3:00 P.M., with no recess break.

Literacy instruction in fifth and sixth grade shared the following components:

- Daily read-aloud.
- Spelling was organized by development. For example, one group began with a review of long vowels; a second group explored how to add affixes to words; and a third group explored the meaning elements of words. Students received their words on Monday and participated in sorting activities through the week. An instructional aide often led word study groups. They had a spelling test on Friday.
- Each student wrote in a journal daily. Most of the entries were guided by a teacher-selected topic.
- Basal texts were used, but the dominant mode of instruction was book club groups. Students read silently or orally, wrote in a literature log, and discussed their reading with other students and the teacher.
- Writing took many forms. Students wrote in learning logs, and wrote stories and informational reports.
- The AR program was used daily.

At the end of the year, teachers were pleased with their students' development, and particularly in fifth grade, with instructional organization. Mrs. Callep said, "We had a dynamic year. We piloted the fifth-grade organization where we shared the kids in all subjects. The high group [in reading] moved way beyond where they normally are—to a higher level of thinking. The grouping helped us focus on individuals." Sixth-grade teachers had similar positive comments.

> Ms. Jones: "Our students cared about each other. They wanted to learn and they let us teach. Rarely did a student disrupt learning. They seemed to enjoy the activities we planned for them."
> Ms. Booth: "This was a smooth year. They are engaged in reading and writing. They are the highest scoring class on the writing assessment I have ever had."
> Mr. McGuire: "The kids were motivated to read. They were easy to teach. I tried book clubs. I have a lot to learn about them, but I saw my students excited about reading."

The fifth- and sixth-grade teachers matched those described by Block and Mangieri (2003) in that they adapted their instruction and organization to meet the needs of individual students. Throughout their day, they each developed content and literacy knowledge in their students as they simultaneously worked on building student self-esteem. Frequently, I saw students stay in at recess or come to school early or stay late to chat with a teacher. Intermediate teachers always seemed to find the time for these important personal chats. Moreover, sixth-grade teachers facilitated a transition from elementary school to middle school by developing a field trip on which sixth-grade students visited the middle school long before entry into it. The teachers were aware of the tension and fear of their students as they prepared for this academic milestone, and they proactively facilitated this transition.

A final comparison can also be made between these teachers and those described by Pressley, Wharton-McDonald, Mistretta-Hampston, and Echevarria (1998), in that they organized students into multiple groupings, developed literal, as well as inferential, thinking through discussion and writing, used a variety of curricular materials, and spent significant time on writing to understand in content areas. Their consistent literacy focus resulted in the majority of students reaching grade-level benchmarks or above and few students that were considered to be struggling readers. This is a huge accomplishment for teachers and students in any school, and particularly in a high-poverty school, where so many students arrived understanding and speaking a language other than English.

COMPARISONS OF EXEMPLARY
AND NOT SO EXEMPLARY PRACTICES

As I observed over 7 years, I noted exemplary instruction and instruction that was not so exemplary (Barone, 2003). For the most part, the not so exemplary instruction occurred when teachers were trying out new practices. By exploring these practices, readers can benefit from the experiences of teachers at Howard. Howard teachers were brave in that they participated in on-site professional development daily. Changing and refining practice were mantras in the school. However, although change was institutionalized, it still was not easy for teachers to sustain change in their classrooms, as shown earlier in this chapter in the example from Mrs. Harter's kindergarten. Although key elements of literacy (phonemic awareness, phonics, comprehension, vocabulary, fluency, and writing) were not as familiar when I started this study, before the National Panel Report, I have used them to organize the practices shared. I have selected practices across grade levels and have not targeted any specific grade level for examples.

Phonemic Awareness

Not So Exemplary

On one of the first days of kindergarten, Mrs. Harter gave each child a card with his or her name on it. She asked children to return their card if their name began with a certain letter. For example, when she said "C," children whose names began with *C* brought her their card. The difficulty with this activity so early in the year is that few children understood English or had any awareness of letter recognition. As a result, Mrs. Harter had to go to each child as she said a letter and collect his or her card, if appropriate. This took a huge amount of time, and few children were able to connect the first letter of their name and the letter the teacher announced.

This activity would have been more successful later in the year, when students had more understanding of English and of letters. The activity is not problematic, just the timing of it.

Exemplary

Mrs. Martin decided to use songs to transition students into kindergarten when they first arrived. At first, children sang nursery rhymes, but toward the end of the year Mrs. Martin used specific songs to focus on rhyming words. For example, in a rendition of *Old MacDonald Had a Farm*, she might sing, "Old MacDonald has a pig and the pig likes to. . . ." Students joined in with *dig*. Students enjoyed this activity, and began to notice rhyming words and comment about them to their teacher.

Phonics

Not So Exemplary

Children in Mrs. Messina and Mrs. Denton's first-grade classroom benefited from a technology grant awarded to these teachers. Because of the grant, they had additional computers and software programs in their classroom. They used computers and software in a center, with Mrs. Messina moving between her reading groups and supervision of the computer center. Not surprisingly, several students found ways to move away from the practice programs that students were expected to use when their teacher was focused on a reading group. One day, as Julio practiced finding pictures that began with certain initial consonants on the computer, he practiced a few minutes, then changed to a game program. Although Julio's ability to change programs is laudable, his practice of phonics is not. Each time I saw him at the computer, he found ways not to engage in the practice programs planned by his teacher.

In this example, the use of technology is not the issue. What is problematic is that Julio's teachers were using software programs for phonics practice, and students like Julio, who were still not consistent on sound–symbol relationships, were not participating. Julio's teacher was stretched between teaching a small group and supervision, and supervision took a second position. Unfortunately, Julio avoided structured practice programs and continued to struggle with letter–sound knowledge throughout the year.

Exemplary

Mr. Shott and Mrs. Sims divided their first-grade class for phonics instruction. While Mr. Shott worked with a group of students on the initial sound of *b*, Mrs. Sims used the word wall to focus on short-*a* words. She began her lesson by having students find all the words with short *a* on the word wall. Students quickly responded with *bat, hat, man,* and so on. Mrs. Sims said, "I knew they knew short *a* because they found the words so quickly." After students found words, she modeled writing the words. She recorded short-*a* words on her chart as students simultaneously wrote them on white boards. Once they had written about 10 words, she asked them if they noticed anything about the words. One child said, "Some have *at* in them." Another child noticed that "some have *an* in them." Students then used a red marker to underline the *an* words and a black marker to underline the *at* words. Before she dismissed her group, Mrs. Sims asked them to take their white boards and see if they could find *an* or *at* words in their book tub books. Later in the day, they reconvened and shared words.

In this lesson, Mrs. Sims used the word wall to target specific words with the short-*a* pattern that she believed students were ready to explore. Once students identified words, she had them write them, then sort them by short *a* and the letter that followed. She did not end her lesson here; she wanted students to take what they learned about short *a* independent of text and move to identifying these words in text. She accomplished several goals in having students return to text: They found other short-*a* words, they sorted them, and they engaged in rereading of familiar text, thus gaining fluency as well.

Comprehension

Not So Exemplary

The following example is from a first-grade classroom. The teacher was working with four students in a guided reading lesson. Students were orally reading *Baby Bear's Present*, a leveled text. Maritza, a member of this group, read orally and had the following dialogue with her teacher:

> MARITZA: (*reading*) Mother Bear says baby bear has no toys. Let's get a toy for Little Teddy.
>
> TEACHER: Little Teddy is incorrect. What is the first letter?
>
> MARITZA: Baby Bear. (*reading*) Let's go to the sit toy.
>
> TEACHER: Reread that.
>
> MARITZA: (*reading*) Let's go to the store today. They looked in the store w . . . (*Maritza looks at the picture in the book*) wind–ow.
>
> TEACHER: Right. Usually that's how it is, but this time it says *o*.
>
> MARITZA: (*reading*) Window. We will look at trains too, said Father Bear. I like trains. I like his train, said Father Bear. This little key macks it go. I can hep Little Teddy.
>
> TEACHER: (*reading*) I can help Little Bear.

This reading and correcting continued throughout the book. At the end, there was no discussion of anything that happened in the story.

Unfortunately, this teacher's single focus was on decoding. In some instances, such as the substitution of Little Teddy for Baby Bear, there were no comprehension issues; Maritza just used another name for the bear. Other words, such as *window, makes,* and *help,* might have caused confusion in meaning getting. Because there was no discussion of text before or after reading, comprehension was never a focus of this reading session. Maritza never learned that mispronunciations resulted in meaning confusion; rather, she learned that getting the words right was the most important part of reading. She also learned that her teacher would supply the correct word when she struggled, and she did not have to decode new words independently. Adams (2001) noted that interrupting beginner readers with a decoding focus results in readers who read slowly and substitute words that do not make sense.

Exemplary

In sixth grade, Anthony and another student were reading *Hatchet* (Paulsen, 1988) in preparation for a meeting they would have with their teacher and their reading group. As Anthony read, he often stopped and chatted with his friend about this book.

> ANTHONY: Look at this. (*He reads a piece of text.*) This is interesting. I think the mother got a divorce because it says, "On Wednesday she went to exercise. Then on Thursday, she went to see him." It sounds like she was forced to go.
>
> BOY: Yes, it sounds like my mom when she sees my dad.
>
> ANTHONY: Oh yeah, I remember this part. I didn't understand it well yesterday. Now it is clearer.
>
> BOTH BOYS: (*They chat about how much weight he will lose by being lost.*)
>
> ANTHONY: If he finds a road he could ask someone. I wouldn't want to keep on walking. This reminds me of *Cast Away* and how he tried to make a fire. Maybe he can hunt birds.

In this brief example, Anthony and his friend demonstrated how they have internalized numerous comprehension strategies taught by their teachers. First, they talked with each other for clarification. Second, they reread when they were confused. Third, they predicted what might happen. Fourth, they used personal knowledge to make sense of text. Finally, they built connections between this book and a movie about being alone on an island. In listening to this informal conversation, I learned much about how these boys internalized the instruction focused on comprehension, taught by their teacher. I found this to be one of the most striking examples of exemplary teaching, because the strategies were automatically used by the students while they were reading independently. Mazzoni and Gambrell (2003) note that "becoming fully literate means being able to use strategies independently to construct meaning" (p. 11).

Vocabulary

Not So Exemplary

Many teachers were aware that not understanding the meaning of words was hampering students' comprehension. This need became particularly evident to Howard's teachers when achievement test scores came back and all of the fourth-grade students had scored low in vocabulary. In sixth grade, Ms. Booth decided to focus on vocabulary to improve student achievement. When she read to the class, or when small groups read novels with her, she frequently stopped and drew students' attention to words and their meanings. Unfortunately, these brief encounters with words did not allow students to make these words truly their own. Following is a short conversation that occurred as students read *True Confessions of Charlotte Doyle* (Avi, 1990):

MS. BOOTH: What is a satanic smirk?

STUDENTS: (*No response.*)

MS. BOOTH: An evil smile. I think she is afraid and imagining how much danger she is in. That is called *foreboding*. What does that mean?

STUDENT: Scary.

MS. BOOTH: (*Continues reading. She stops reading and inserts:*) *Grotesque* means *distorted*. What does *distorted* mean?

STUDENT: Messed up.

Students continued reading, and Ms. Booth continued to draw their attention to words. The result of this instruction was threefold: Students struggled with comprehension, reading was fragmented and lacked fluency, and students did not understand or remember the vocabulary. Certainly, Ms. Booth's intentions were correct, but comprehension was hampered by students' lack of vocabulary knowledge; therefore, her strategy to teach vocabulary was ineffective. Students needed a more systematic approach to learn vocabulary, one in which the words became their own (see Beck, McKeown, & Kucan, 2002).

Exemplary

Mrs. Callep, a fourth-grade teacher, had a word jar—a large jar with word cards in it—in her room. Students contributed words to it, and Mrs. Callep added words from reading, social studies, or science. Each day, one word was selected, and students discussed it and used it throughout the day. On a day that I was observing, Heidee selected the word *kaleidoscope*. She read the word and waited for support from her teacher.

> MRS. CALLEP: Does anyone have one?
>
> HEIDEE: I think you see stars through it and the planets.
>
> MRS. CALLEP: I think you might be thinking of another word.
>
> STUDENT: Microscope?
>
> MRS. CALLEP: Does anyone know what scope means?
>
> STUDENT: Something to look through?
>
> MRS. CALLEP: That's right.
>
> STUDENT: I have a kaleidoscope at home and I look at the stars.
>
> MRS. CALLEP: I think we might have a telescope and a kaleidoscope confused.
>
> STUDENT: I get it. I use a telescope to see the stars.
>
> MRS. CALLEP: We still aren't sure what a kaleidoscope is, so when we are done reading, can someone look it up for us and report back?

Later a child reported on what a kaleidoscope is. The students were still interested in words with *scope* in them, so the teacher worked with a group of students to create a chart with *scope* words. Once they had a list, they collaborated on the meaning of each word.

In this example, the teacher developed a lesson based on confusion over the meaning of a word. She took the opportunity to explore a root and learn its meaning in a multitude of words. Students generated this meaning across words rather than learning each word as an isolate. Later they were able to decipher the meaning of any word with the root *scope* in it.

Fluency

Not So Exemplary

Overall, there was not much instruction directed toward word fluency in any of the grades. In one lesson I observed in second grade, students were working in a small group with their teacher. Each student selected a book to reread, one that had been read in previous small-group sessions. Jaryd chose the book *Lunch with Cat and Dog* (a leveled text). Jaryd's teacher listened in as he read this book orally to her. He struggled over numerous words, such as *chocolate*, *begged*, and *screamed*. His teacher helped him sound out each of these words. When Jaryd guessed *surprised* for *screamed*, his teacher said, "Look at the picture and see what she is doing." Jaryd replied, "Smiled." His teacher then had him focus on the *sc* to decode *screamed*. Immediately following Jaryd's reading, he was directed to reread this book with another student in the group.

His teacher knew that rereading would help Jaryd decode this book more readily, and help with comprehension and fluency. Unfortunately, Jaryd reread this book with another student and continuously stumbled over multiple words. Although this book may have been instructionally appropriate, it was too difficult for Jaryd to read independently. Even after rereading this book three times, Jaryd continued to stumble over many words on each page; thus, he never gained fluency reading this text. Maybe if he had engaged in similar practice with this book over several days his fluency would have improved. Unfortunately, this was not the case.

His teacher recognized that rereading was a good strategy to build fluency. What was neglected was finding text that a student could read independently and sustain this practice over several days. Without a focus on matching a text to a student's current knowledge, rereading did not lead to more fluency; rather, Jaryd became frustrated with the task and abandoned it.

Exemplary

I have selected two exemplary practices to support fluency. The first one is with a small group of end-of-the-year first graders. They read the poem *Miss Mary Mack* together, with support from their teacher. After this initial reading, the teacher broke students up by partners, who read the poem to each other. When the teacher regrouped them, all students chorally read the poem once more. Then, to continue building fluency, the teacher gave each student an envelope that contained each line from the poem written on sentence strips. Students were dismissed to work with a partner to reassemble the poem. As students completed the reassembly, they constantly reread the poem and gained fluency with it.

The second example comes from a second-grade classroom. An instructional aide worked with students on a Readers' Theatre script of *Little Red Riding Hood*. The children and the aide read through the play together with the aide stopping periodically to help with words that students struggled over, such as *caught*. This was all they completed on the first day. The next day, the aide revisited the play and quickly read it with students. She then assigned parts to individual students, and they practiced. This routine continued throughout the week, with students performing the play at the end of the week. Students enjoyed this activity and developed fluency (Allington, 2001).

As shared in both examples, students had multiple opportunities to engage in purposeful rereading. These practices allowed them to experience fluent reading and to deepen their comprehension as well.

Writing

Not So Exemplary

In many of the classrooms, teachers spent about 30 minutes each day devoted to DOL activities. Students copied sentences from the board and attempted to correct spelling, capitalization, and punctuation errors independently. Once students completed their corrections, teachers worked with the whole class to review corrections. Students were then expected to correct these errors on their papers. As I watched this instruction, students rarely, if ever, corrected mistakes after whole-class correction. A few students in each room actively engaged in this process, while the majority of students passively listened or paid no attention.

These explicit lessons on grammar, spelling, and punctuation were never embedded in the writing students completed. They always remained a separate activity, not tied to student work. I often wondered why teachers did not select students' examples for the class to correct. This simple change would have connected the instruction to student editing. Perhaps students would then have seen the value of these corrections.

Exemplary

Mr. McGuire and Ms. Jones engaged sixth graders in writing for many purposes each day. (These teachers shared their students for instruction.) During math and science lessons, Ms. Jones had students record their current understandings. She used these jottings informally to assess students' current knowledge and any misunderstandings they might have to guide future lessons. Mr. McGuire supported students in formal and informal writing. During the literacy block, students wrote in journals and in response to their reading. He also supported students in writing workshop to develop longer pieces of writing that were sometimes narrative and other times informational. While students wrote, Mr. McGuire conferred with them or worked on his own story, a book about sixth graders. He often asked students to listen to what he had written, so that he might improve it. His students were always willing to help him, particularly when he did not represent them accurately in his book.

One day, I listened in as he began writing workshop:

MR. MCGUIRE: I noticed how you are inserting important details in your writing. Can you tell me about your strategies for doing this?

MARITZA: I brainstorm and put them in a web.

ERIC: I write some details down and then I add when I think of others.

JARYD: I just make a list.

MR. MCGUIRE: These are important ways to include details. Today, when I walk around the room, I want you to show me how you decide on what details to include.

The students got out their writing from the previous day, and many reread and continued to write. Mr. McGuire visited almost every student and chatted about including details. He took notes, he said, so that "I can share your strategies with other students."

When I looked at a few papers, it was evident to me that students were including details to support their opinions. An example of Jaryd's writing follows:

Being a good student will help my future. All I have to do is work and put my heart and soul into my work. Another way is to listen to the feelings inside of me that tell me to do what is right. The third thing is to listen to the teacher. You should always listen to the one who is talking. If you help someone they will help you. The fourth thing is to share and then the other students will share with you. . . .

Although Jaryd's writing certainly needs revision, he has included many details that will help him be a better student. When they conferred, Jaryd showed Mr. McGuire the list that he created, with all of his reasons about being a good student. He said, "I thought of a lot of reasons and then the kids at the table helped me think of more. Now I am writing them."

Mr. McGuire's teaching practice supports his student writers in that he provides time each day for formal and informal writing—"Writing is something you learn and writing is used to learn." He validates his students by learning about their strategies and recording them to share with future students. Finally, he engages his students in private conversations about their writing to support each of them personally and foster their writing development.

ELL Support

I have chosen not to include "not so exemplary" examples here, because so many teachers totally ignored any support for ELLs. No support serves as the "not so exemplary" example. While it is unfortunate that the students at Howard did not benefit from explicit support of their home language or culture, these teachers are not unlike others, for they had received little in the way of professional development to support ELLs (Beykont, 2002; Carrasquillo & Rodriguez, 2002). However, sometimes teachers explicitly supported the language needs of their students, as illustrated in several examples that follow.

In second grade, Julio talked to his teacher about a book he was reading. Julio tried to tell his teacher that he wanted to be a photographer like the one in the book, but he was unsure of the word in English. He stopped the conversation and went over to a more proficient ELL student to talk with him in Spanish to discover the word—*photographer*. Julio then returned to his teacher to share this word and to continue their conversation. Mrs. Smith stopped all instruction in the classroom to highlight the strategy that Julio used to discover this word. She said, "Julio just struggled with an English word, *photographer*, so he went to Eduardo to get help. Eduardo told him the word, and now Julio knows it. I love seeing how you can use two languages so well." This brief example demonstrates how a teacher supported connections between the home language, Spanish, and the school language, English. Following up on this event, students created a chart that compared English and Spanish words, and frequently added to this classroom resource.

A second example comes from Mrs. Scott's fourth-grade classroom. Mrs. Scott read novels to students daily. In September, she chose a book about Mexican Independence Day. Before she started to read, she asked her students to help her with unfamiliar vocabulary. In this way, she made students whose home language was Spanish the experts. A bit of discussion from the first day of reading in this book follows:

> BONNIE: I celebrated Independence Day in El Salvador. My mom was born there.
>
> MRS. SCOTT: Yes, we usually only talk about the U.S. becoming independent, but other countries have independence days too. (*Reads and stops.*) I don't know what this word means. I will write it on the board: *mestizos*. I am not sure, so after I finish reading this part, we will talk about what it might mean. Listen as I read to see if you can figure it out.

In this example, the teacher purposely selected a book that connected to students' background knowledge and language. Students became the experts in language—vocabulary—and contributed a variety of information about independence days. Through the selection of this book, students were valued and were able to connect a variety of independence days to their study of America's independence.

The last example comes from a third-grade classroom. Mrs. Walker often had students look up words when they were confused about their meaning. She had a wide variety of dictionaries available for students. I often saw students look up the same word in different dictionaries to see whether the dictionaries agreed. During the year, Mrs. Walker added Spanish–English dictionaries to her collection. One day, Maria and Eric were looking up the word *nation* to find a definition for their reading group. They checked the Spanish–English dictionary and found *nación* and made the connection between these words. Later, in their reading group, they shared this information.

Students then routinely compared cognates in Spanish and English, and language became a focus of study.

FINAL THOUGHTS

Looking across teaching from kindergarten through sixth grade, there is no doubt that teachers at Howard worked diligently to facilitate the reading and writing development of their students. Although many strategies were incorporated into their instruction, perhaps the most dominant was grouping students, so that they could target instruction to current levels of literacy knowledge. Mrs. Katen said, "I like the literacy block and only working with kids kind of at the same level. They weren't so diverse. I had more time to focus on individuals." This targeted focus facilitated student achievement, as noted in end-of-sixth-grade achievement. These students were able to beat the fourth-grade slump and comprehend text that was more abstract and difficult (Chall, Jacobs, & Baldwin, 1990). Moreover, while ELLs typically fail to reach benchmark levels at the end of elementary school, only one ELL focal student did not reach this level at Howard (Drucker, 2003).

Teachers also began to look seriously at assessment data and revise instruction to meet needs of students (e.g., as in vocabulary). Additionally, during the last year of my study, teachers reconstructed their onsite professional development to focus on ELLs and how to reconfigure instruction to support their learning. Teachers at Howard constantly looked at school data and inward, at their own practices, to better support their students' learning.

While it is always easy to find ways that instruction could have been better, these teachers were dedicated to improving their instruction. This is not to say that changing familiar instruction methods was easy for them. They often abandoned new strategies or merged old strategies into the new ones. For instance, when introducing book clubs, they had students read orally to each other in a round-robin fashion. What is most important in considering this long-term view of teaching at a high-poverty school is that these teachers constantly tried to meet the learning needs of their students. They saw themselves as students as they explored together current best practices in literacy.

Moreover, many of the teachers, particularly intermediate teachers, built personal relationships with students and had high expectations of them. Their relationship building and expectations made a difference in students' end-of-elementary-school achievement.

REFERENCES

Adams, M. J. (2001). Alphabetic anxiety and explicit, systematic phonics instruction: A cognitive science perspective. In S. B. Neuman & D. K. Dickinson (Eds.), *Handbook of early literacy research* (Vol. 1, pp. 66–80). New York: Guilford Press.

Allington, R. (2001). *What really matters for struggling readers: Designing research-based programs.* New York: Longman.

Avi. (1990). *True confessions of Charlotte Doyle.* New York: Avon Books.

Barone, D. (2002a). Literacy teaching and learning in two kindergarten classrooms in a school labeled at-risk. *Elementary School Journal, 102,* 415–441.

Barone, D. (2002b). Learning and teaching at an at-risk school. *Literacy Teaching and Learning, 6*(2), 1–42.

Barone, D. (2003). Caution, apply with care: Recommendations for early literacy instruction. In D. Barone & L. Morrow (Eds.), *Literacy and young children: Research-based practices* (pp. 291–308). New York: Guilford Press.

Bear, D., Invernizzi, M., Templeton, S., & Johnston, F. (2004). *Words their way: Word study for phonics, vocabulary, and spelling instruction* (3rd ed.). Upper Saddle River, NJ: Prentice-Hall.

Beck, I. L., McKeown, M. G., & Kucan, L. (2002). *Bringing words to life: Robust vocabulary instruction.* New York: Guilford Press.

Beykont, Z. (2002). Introduction. In *The power of culture* (pp. vii–xxxvi). Cambridge, MA: Harvard Education Publishing.

Block, C. C., & Mangieri, J. N. (2003). *Exemplary literacy teachers: Promoting success for all children in grades K–5.* New York: Guilford Press.

Brown, D. (2002). *Becoming a successful urban teacher.* Portsmouth, NH: Heinemann.

Carrasquillo, A., & Rodriguez, V. (2002). *Language minority students in the mainstream classroom* (2nd ed.). Philadelphia: Multilingual Matters.

Chall, J., Jacobs, V., & Baldwin, L. (1990). *The reading crisis: Why poor children fall behind.* Cambridge, MA: Harvard University Press.

Drucker, M. (2003). What reading teachers should know about ESL learners. *Reading Teacher, 57,* 22–29.

Gutierrez, K., Basquedano-Lopez, P., & Turner, M. (1997). Putting language back into language arts: When the radical middle meets the third space. *Language Arts, 74,* 368–378.

Johnson, P. (2004). *Choice words: How our language affects children's learning.* Portland, ME: Stenhouse.

Ladson-Billings, G. (1994). *The dreamkeepers: Successful teachers of African American children.* San Francisco: Jossey-Bass.

Mazzoni, S. A., & Gambrell, L. B. (2003). Principles of best practice: Finding the common ground. In L. M. Morrow, L. B. Gambrell, & M. Pressley (Eds.), *Best practices in literacy instruction* (2nd ed., pp. 9–21). New York: Guilford Press.

Meier, T. (2003). "Why can't she remember that?": The importance of storybook reading in multilingual, multicultural classrooms. *Reading Teacher, 57,* 242–252.

National Reading Panel. (2000). *Teaching children to read: An evidence-based assessment of the scientific research literature on reading and its implications for reading instruction: Reports of the subgroups.* Washington, DC: National Institute of Child Health and Human Development.

Paulsen, G. (1988). *Hatchet.* New York: Simon & Schuster.

Pressley, M., Wharton-McDonald, R., Mistretta-Hampston, J., & Echevarria, M. (1998). Literacy instruction in 10 grade fourth- and fifth-grade classrooms in upstate New York. *Scientific Study of Reading, 2,* 159–194.

Reglin, G. (1995). *Achievement for African-American students: Strategies for the diverse classroom.* Bloomington, IN: National Educational Service.

Reutzel, D. R. (2003). Organizing effective literacy instruction: Grouping strategies and instructional routines. In L. M. Morrow, L. B. Gambrell, & M. Pressley (Eds.), *Best practices in literacy instruction* (2nd ed, pp. 241–267). New York: Guilford Press.

Taylor, B., Pearson, P. D., Clark, K., & Walpole, S. (1999). Effective schools/accomplished teachers. *Reading Teacher, 53,* 156–159.

Waxman, H., Padrón, Y., & Gray, J. (2004). *Educational resiliency: Student, teacher, and school perspectives.* Greenwich, CN: Information Age.

Yopp, H.K., & Yopp, R.H. (2000). Supporting phonemic awareness development in the classroom. *Reading Teacher, 54,* 130–143.

Chapter 4

Widening the Lens

*Multiple Perspectives on
Teaching and Learning*

Children reorganize and rearticulate their resources and,
in the process, they may differentiate and expand their
knowledge about symbolic systems, social practices, and
the ideologically complex world. In this view of
development, the children do not move in step along a
narrow literacy path but, at least ideally, more
deliberately maneuver on an expanding landscape.
—ANNE HAAS DYSON (2003, p. 15)

This quotation frames the nonlinear view of children's literacy development explored in this chapter. I have chosen three lenses to extend the more linear literacy perspective of students and teachers presented in earlier chapters. Each lens adds to an understanding of the students and their literacy experiences. Taken together, they offer a layered, multifaceted understanding of students as they learned to read and write.

The first lens, social constructivism, affords a view into the social dynamic of classrooms and how teachers encouraged or did not encourage academic community building within their rooms (Almasi, 2002; Enciso, 1996; Gee, 2001). Through viewing with this lens, we can study students' creation of knowledge as they talked about and through developing understandings.

The second lens, positioning theory (Harré & Langenhove, 1999), is used to open up the power dynamic that appeared in classrooms as teachers and students negotiated their student and teacher identities. Through this lens, the structure of classroom learning and how it helped or hindered student learning becomes evident.

The final lens is resilience theory (Benard, 2004). Students in Howard often demonstrated their resilience as they successfully managed their out-of-school lives while negotiating their elementary school curriculum. This perspective allows for an understanding of individual strengths of students and teachers in supporting their learning.

Each of these lenses provides a unique way of interpreting the experiences of students and teachers. What one lens reveals another conceals. For example, by considering the social dynamic to learning, resiliency is not explored explicitly and moves to the background. These views, coupled with the earlier discussion of learning and teaching, provide a more complete exploration of these students as they navigated their elementary literacy experiences.

SOCIAL-CONSTRUCTIVIST PERSPECTIVE

Both high and low achieving students of all backgrounds
expressed a strong preference for working in groups because it
helped them generate ideas and participate actively in class.
—SONIA NIETO (2002, p. 135)

The social-constructivist perspective has been notably highlighted in the work of Nieto in her study of ELLs and Dyson in her exploration of young student writers. Dyson (1993) observed that there was a sense of identification and connection among teachers and students in dialogic classrooms. She believed that classrooms in successful schools were rich in conversation, with space for student choice to influence the teacher's plans. For example, if a student explored a superhero in writing, the teacher supported this exploration in positive ways rather than restricting the topic.

Whereas Dyson studied in an exemplary classroom, classroom communities vary dramatically in the way teachers structure their classrooms to match their teaching philosophy (e.g., from classrooms in which children are quiet and expected to work in isolation to classrooms that foster academic conversation among students). Although teachers have this authority, research supports student learning in language-rich environments. For instance, Wilkinson and Silliman (2000) argue that students should have extensive opportunities "for the integration of oral and written language in the classroom, because these experiences both support and encourage literate cognition" (p. 337). Additionally, Purcell-Gates, McIntyre, and Freppon (1995) document that children from high-poverty backgrounds gain knowledge of written narrative more successfully in classrooms that emphasize more holistic uses and functions of language. In these classrooms, conversations among students, and among students and teachers, are seen as critical to student achievement and understanding.

With this background in mind, I reanalyzed the data to explore the way teachers encouraged or limited students' collaborative learning. Unfortunately, across many of the grades and classrooms, teachers expected students to be quiet, unless called upon, and to work independently. However, in some classrooms, teachers supported the collaborative nature of learning and fostered student engagement in academic topics on some occasions.

Although it is easy to be critical of such quiet teaching and learning, I endeavored to find reasons why teachers made this choice. I heard from some teachers that their primary concern was to have students behave and conform to school expectations. The result of this goal was that students talked when called upon. One third-grade teacher confirmed this focus on behavior when she told me, "The principal gave me a glowing evaluation because my class is quiet." Another possible reason was that teachers tried to maximize learning time. They believed that they needed to accelerate the learning of students in an academic year, so that they met grade-level expectations. A second-grade teacher explained, "They lose so much over the summer. They always come back at least six months behind. I have to make sure they gain back that six months and grow a whole academic year as well. So I teach them directly to maximize our time in school." Other teachers related that they were worried about test results. A result of this worry was explicit, direct teaching. Their hope was that students would do better on achievement tests with this direct approach. When I consider these reasons and others not overtly mentioned by teachers, it is not surprising that students most often learned in quiet environments, where learning was an individual endeavor. Messier, conversation-based learning took time, complicated classroom management, and was not directly tested; as a result, this kind of learning infrequently dominated classroom environments.

Read-Aloud in First Grade

The first example is from the first-grade classroom of Mr. Shott and Mrs. Sims. Each morning, one of these teachers led students in a discussion of a read-aloud book in a corner of the room comfortably arranged for listening (Wolf, 2004). These teachers often organized their read-alouds by theme, author, or illustrator. They believed that children's comprehension and vocabulary developed through these read-alouds, particularly when they organized books to build connections across them.

One day, I closely watched the interaction among the students and between Mr. Shott and his students as he read a *Clifford* book (Bridwell). Mr. Shott engaged his students in exploration of all of the *Clifford* books and had a table in the room with multiple *Clifford* books on it. He began his conversation by asking students if they had found additional *Clifford* books in the library, thus demonstrating connections between learning in school and out of school:

MR. SHOTT: Did anyone find more *Clifford* books in the library?

MARIA: I looked, but I only found the ones we have.

JOHN: I didn't find them in the library, but I brought one that I had at home. Can you read it?

MR. SHOTT: I can, but first let's talk about Clifford. What's unusual about Clifford?

DIEGO: He's big.

CHRISTINA: He's red.

MR. SHOTT: He has two things that are different. He is big and red like an apple. I think he would have a hard time playing hide and seek, don't you?

STUDENTS: I can find him.

MR. SHOTT: (*Begins to read book and then stops.*) The dog is in the tent. Is he angry? How can you tell?

MARIA: He smells something.

TAMEKA: I think it is the hot dogs.

CHRIS: I don't think he's angry, just hungry.

MR. SHOTT: (*Continues reading.*)

CHRIS: He's begging.

MARIA: My dog does that. My mom gets mad.

TAMEKA: So does mine. Sometimes he sneaks food.

MR. SHOTT: (*Continues reading.*)

TAMEKA: Look at that mountain lion.

MARIA: He looks scared.

MR. SHOTT: (*Continues reading.*)

CHRIS: He is crying.

MR. SHOTT: I am not sure he is crying, but he does look sad.

STUDENTS: (*Overlapping conversation as the children discuss whether Clifford is sad.*)

MR. SHOTT: (*Finishes book.*) Well, that was the introduction to Clifford and Emily.

Following from this initial reading, the students continued to chat with Mr. Shott and among themselves about what else they knew about Emily and Clifford. The students understood that Mr. Shott valued their comments and ideas about books. This simple picture book resulted in numerous, spontaneous discussions throughout the reading. Mr. Shott dismissed his students from this read-aloud, although they continued to explore Clifford books. From his book reading, they went to a table, where they perused other Clifford books to learn more about Emily and Clifford. Students worked together on a chart, where they added characteristics about them. For the next half-hour, students chatted about Clifford and Emily, with some children just considering the illustrations and others reading text to be used on their charts.

Importantly, Mr. Shott encouraged his students in conversation about this book as he read. Students built on the comments of others, as is seen in the snippet of dialogue shared above. Furthermore, Mr. Shott extended this academic conversation by requesting that students chat and explore other *Clifford* books to find additional details about these characters. He knew that for his class of almost all students new to English, extended time with multiple books about a few characters allowed his students to discuss the books he read in authentic ways. During each additional read-aloud, he "watched to see that all students participated, even the quiet ones."

Mr. Shott's and Mrs. Sims's focus on talk about literature was important to these young learners in a multitude of ways. First, these students learned about the characters, setting, and plot in narratives; second, they used academic language in their discussions (most were ELLs, and they readily participated in conversations about books); third, they interpreted illustrations and text, and went beyond literal comprehension; fourth, although not shown in the above-mentioned example, they explored informational text and learned about its organizational structures and how to gain information from them; and fifth, students made connections across books and learned about authors and illustrators.

Sloan (1991), more formally, also recognized the importance of talk surrounding read-alouds in developing deeper comprehension and interpretation of text. She wrote:

> Time for purposeful talk after the experiences of literature is analogous to the lab after a presentation in science. It is time for experimenting with ideas, exploring concepts, making observations, and drawing conclusions. . . . From their first encounter with a new class, teachers need to work to establish a climate of mutual respect where ideas and opinions are heard and valued. (pp. 132–133)

Although Mr. Shott and Mrs. Sims may not have been familiar with the research conducted by Sloan, they certainly actualized the important ideas she shared in this work in their classroom. They understood implicitly and explicitly that talk focused on comprehension and vocabulary supported their young students in learning to read and write.

Although this example may appear to be routine, I infrequently saw this open dialogue about reading in classrooms. Typically, teachers moved through books at a rapid pace and only engaged students in teacher-generated questions. A single student responded, and the teacher continued reading. Or the teacher asked a question about a word's meaning, and if a student could not provide a definition, the teacher provided one and continued reading. In Mr. Shott's and Mrs. Sims's room, students routinely participated in rich discussion centered on reading. During the day, it was common to observe children chatting with one of their teachers or fellow students about a new discovery or question they had about reading. Academic talk about books and their meaning permeated this classroom and the students within it.

Writing Workshop in Third Grade

The second example comes from a third-grade classroom. Mrs. Erin organized her room to include a writing workshop that students experienced daily. During this workshop, it was common to hear students chat about a topic they were writing about, revising, and/or editing. One day, I listened in as Josie composed a piece about her sister's new dog. She worked with Chakela, and they conversed about dogs as Josie wrote. Some of their conversation follows:

> JOSIE: I'm writing about my sister's dog. What are you writing about?
>
> CHAKELA: I don't know. I am looking at my work to see if I can get an idea. I think I'm out of ideas today (*skimming through her writing folder*).
>
> JOSIE: Maybe you should write about a dog too. Do you have one?
>
> CHAKELA: We did, but it's dead.

JOSIE: What do you want to do?

CHAKELA: I can listen to your story.

JOSIE: (*reading*) Two months ago my sister got a Chihuahua.

CHAKELA: How did you know how to spell it? That's hard.

JOSIE: I had to look it up on the Internet. I couldn't figure it out, and I didn't find it in the dictionary. (*Continues reading.*) My sister named her Misty.

CHAKELA: So I know the dog's name but not your sister's. Shouldn't you tell that? What else are you going to say about the dog? Does she carry it in a basket? Is it nice?

This conversation continued as Josie added to her story. While Chakela never began a story that day, she helped Josie frame hers. The following is Josie's completed first draft:

Two months ago my sister got a Chihuahua. My sister name her Misty. Sandy's Chihuahua is black and eys brown sharp teeth and it is a mini Chihuahua Sometimes it bite. She eats dog food and is a girl and in the summer she swims. [not corrected]

When Josie finished this draft, she again read it to Chakela. Chakela asked, "I like the story, but I want to know more about the Chihuahua. Is she just black? How did she think of the name? Does she sleep with you?"

The girls continued to work on this story until Josie shared it with the class. They formed a partnership in writing and routinely helped each other with ideas, revision, and editing throughout their third-grade year. They often completed their final drafts sitting together at the classroom computers. Although in some rooms, teachers formally allow times for peer revision and editing, these girls informally learned from each other daily, with no designated times for each expectation.

Josie and Chakela were not the only students in this room who worked together. Each day, during the writing workshop, students worked alone, with a partner or small group of students, or with their teacher. Mrs. Erin was able to maintain this more complex organizational structure and simultaneously have students engaged in writing or improving their writing. She fluctuated between having students write on their own topic, as shown earlier, or write on a more structured report type of writing. Whatever the topic of writing, students were always encouraged to learn from each other.

When I observed in this classroom, students always appeared to be on-task and engaged in their writing. I asked Mrs. Erin how she had her students maintain this focus everyday. She answered:

> "It is not so easy. I work with them and keep moving around the room to keep them focused on writing. At the beginning, they just put anything down and said 'finished.' We just keep working at it each day. I know they are getting better. I just hope that all this writing, revision, and editing shows up in test results. If not, I don't know if I can keep 1 hour each day for writing. The literacy coach might say I have to focus more on specific skills."

Although Mrs. Erin believed in the importance of process writing and daily time for writing, she worried about carryover to test performance. This tension was evident in many of our informal conversations throughout the year. Although her test scores were okay in relation to the other classes in the school, she continued to fret about them and how her instruction might hinder better student scores.

Sixth-Grade Book Club Reading

Mr. McGuire started the year with very teacher-led small groups of students reading novels. He was not happy with this teacher-dominant approach, so he worked with the intermediate literacy coach to shift to more independent student, book club groups. In this transition, he used spinners that the students spun; then, depending on where the spinner pointed, students summarized, made personal connections, talked about a character, or engaged in some other specific task related to their reading. After students demonstrated their ability and eagerness to talk about their reading, he moved to more open-ended conversations about reading that did not require the use of a spinner to narrow conversation.

In the next example, several students were reading *Hatchet* (Paulsen, 1987), the book chosen by this group, and others were reading books about survival as part of a thematic study that culminated with a field trip to the mountains to learn about survival. There was conversation within the groups and among groups about survival and, in particular, how they would negotiate snow in the mountains.

In this example, Mr. McGuire joined the group as they were completing a discussion of a section of the book.

MR. MCGUIRE: So what is the main problem in this story?

ANTHONY: His parents are divorced.

SANDRA: The pilot gets a heart attack.

MICHAEL: He gets stranded.

MR. MCGUIRE: So he has lots of problems. What do you think he will do? (*Leaves the group to ponder this question.*)

SANDRA: I think he will visit his dad later. First he has to get safe.

ANTHONY: He wants to see his mom and dad.

MICHAEL: He wants to survive in the wilderness.

SANDRA: I think the pilot was weird. He got on the plane with a hatchet.

MICHAEL: They wouldn't let me get on with a hatchet today. They took my dad's razor when we went on a plane.

RAMON: (*Tells a long story about an airplane incident.*)

MICHAEL: Look at this. The pilot is having a heart attack and the plane crashed.

SANDRA: I was scared when I read that. Then he was in a coma.

ANTHONY: I think I would have tried to land the plane.

SANDRA: Maybe I could have used the radio and called for help.

MICHAEL: I would jump out of the window.

This conversation continued; then, this group completed the chapter and again stopped to discuss.

In this conversation, students understood the multiple plots within the story. As the story progressed, Anthony paid most attention to the relationship between Brian and his parents. Sandra was most interested in what happened after the crash. And Michael and Ramon were most concerned about how Brian survived. Even though these students all read the same book, they came away with different understandings that were enriched by listening to the comments of others.

Mr. McGuire enjoyed listening to his students' conversations about books. He said, "I think I controlled too much at the beginning. When I listened in, I found that they had important things to say to each other. Sometimes they get silly, but I keep moving and try to keep them focused." I asked him if he worried about test scores and his more open, conversational approach to support reading. He replied, "We don't have standardized tests in sixth grade, so I don't have to worry about that. We have AR tests, though, and my students are doing well. They have goals each quarter, so I know they are developing."

His response, unlike Mrs. Erin's, indicates that without a grade-level achievement test, he had more freedom to engage students in a more conversation-based curriculum. However, he balanced this more open approach with time each day for AR reading and quizzes—a very individualized process devoid of conversation. He used the quizzes to document student growth as readers.

These two last examples demonstrate the serious, thoughtful conversations students can have about their reading and writing. In both examples, students maintained an academic focus even when their teachers were not present. They moved beyond just completing tasks, because they were required to be truly engaged with the reading and writing activities supported in the classroom community. It is also evident through listening in on their conversations that students were creating personal meaning through their social involvement with peers and their teachers. They built upon the ideas shared by fellow students and refined or extended them.

In addition, the increased social structure for learning created by their teachers did not result in out-of-control students or students who did not do well on norm-referenced achievement tests. Although this structure was not as direct as explicit teaching, students learned and met the benchmark expectations as seen in Table 2.1.

POSITIONING THEORY PERSPECTIVE

Students' attitudes toward literacy seemed to be shaped by the classroom contexts and also by their relationships with the teachers.
—SARAH J. MCCARTHEY (2002, p. 29)

Positioning theory is " the study of local moral orders as ever-shifting patterns of mutual and contestable rights and obligations of speaking and acting" (Harré & van Langenhove, 1999, p. 1). This sounds complicated, but in reality, all people engage in positioning when they enter into conversations or activities with others. For example, at one moment, a person may be an expert; in the next, a novice; and perhaps in another, a collegial partner. Positioning is never a permanent condition, in that the way we are positioned by others, or the way we position ourselves, constantly varies according to the differing circumstances or contexts in which we find ourselves (Harré & van Langenhove, 1999). The shifting nature of positioning then results in participants potentially experiencing comfort, conflict, or discomfort in the positions they assume or are placed in. Through positioning, participants experience a multilayered identity instead of a unitary sense of self (Harré & Gillett, 1994).

Although positioning theory seems distant from the study of literacy development, Dillon (2000) provided further descriptions of this theory and offered a way of connecting it to literacy. Dillon stated "These multiple and shifting identities are understood by thinking about how people position themselves—the way they act and interact with others—and the ways they are positioned by others during interactions—the ways they act based on the messages they get from others and society in general" (p. 137). McCarthey (2002) echoed these thoughts by describing the way students' attitudes toward literacy are shaped by the relationships or positions they enact with their teachers. The idea of these various positions and shifting identities can be observed in a multitude of situations that include classrooms and the persons that function in them. One example in which positioning theory was used to understand literacy was a study conducted by Evans (1996), who used positioning theory to better understand equity in peer-led discussions of literature in a fifth-grade classroom.

The following example should clarify the use of positioning theory as a lens to further understanding of literacy learning and instruction: A teacher tells students that they must create a web before they begin their personal narratives. As this teacher moves through the classroom, he notices that Mandy has not created a web; rather, she has used a chart that has two columns—one for good events and the other for bad events. When Mandy's teacher approaches her, he does not say, "You need to create a web like I directed." He chats with her to learn about her organizational strategy. In this example, Mandy's teacher relinquishes his position of power and shifts to a collegial, equal partnership with one of his students. He listens in to see how her chart supports her writing endeavor.

For this section, rather than choosing multiple examples as I did in the previous section, I decided to focus on one student, Anthony, to understand positioning theory better and how it informs literacy development. Anthony was the most explicit in the positions he assumed in relation to his teachers and the positions his teachers took in relation to him. As I observed in his classrooms, Anthony was unambiguous in his words and actions about his relationships with his teachers. When his teachers were authoritarian and definitely assumed a position of leadership without building personal relationships with students, Anthony rebelled against his supposed position of obedient student. For Anthony, learning was all about the relationships he and his teachers established. Without a personal relationship, Anthony was belligerent and attempted to disrupt teaching and learning in his classroom. His trajectory in literacy learning was often influenced by his shifts in positions.

Kindergarten

Anthony entered kindergarten as one of a few students speaking English and easily understanding the general expectations of the classroom. He was also one of the few children who attended preschool; in addition, he had a mother who frequently read to him. Unlike many children at the beginning of the year, he could write his name, and he knew the alphabet.

Anthony attended kindergarten with two teachers who taught on different days. Anthony presented a very different identity, as demonstrated through the positions he assumed depending on which teacher was present in the room. If Mrs. Martin was teaching, he was resistant to her instruction and infrequently conformed. If she read a story, he moved to the back of the group and talked to other children, pushed, or tugged at them. He did not stop until the teacher intervened. During small groups, he sat but did not complete any of the worksheets. He spent his whole time talking to students sitting near him. Anthony caused Mrs. Martin great frustration as he delayed her goal of covering her curriculum. In this way, Anthony gained power, and he continued to seek this power even when his behavior resulted in punishment. Willis (1977), Foley (1990), and Dressman (1997) have also described students who challenged their teacher's authority through resistance.

Mrs. Martin expressed her frustration with Anthony when she said, "He never listens. All he wants to do is talk. I hate it when he gets the other kids off-task. I know he is smart, but he needs to behave. He is at the principal's office almost every day. I just don't know what to do with him."

When Mrs. George was teaching, Anthony was engaged. He sat in the front when she read and constantly commented to her about the story. She responded by telling him, "You are the smartest child in this room." And whereas students were expected to raise their hands to gain the floor, Anthony was allowed to just blurt out whenever he pleased, as long as his comments related to the story. After reading or chatting with students, Mrs. George sat at her desk while her students worked at tables. On most days, Anthony was at her desk five to 10 times during independent working time just to chat with her. While other students were sent back to their table, Mrs. George privileged Anthony by conversing with him. Anthony's relationship was with his teacher, not with the other students in this room, and Mrs. George had a special relationship with Anthony that was not available to other students.

Mrs. George discussed Anthony by saying, "He is really smart. I know he won't have any trouble in school. I love talking to him. He is one of the few kids who knows what is going on." Her comments are certainly different from Mrs. Martin's. The disparate comments also suggested that these teachers did not confer about curriculum or the students for which they were responsible. As Anthony realized, his kindergarten experience was really two experiences, depending on the days of the week.

Anthony was fortunate that he had home literacy experiences, preschool literacy experiences, and kindergarten literacy instruction to draw upon as he developed as a reader and writer. Despite his negative experiences 2 days each week, he left kindergarten as one of the most proficient students in literacy skills.

First Grade

Anthony arrived in first grade with two very separate school identities in place—identities based on the relationships established with his teachers. He could be a compliant student, albeit a very special one, if he was recognized by his teacher, or he could be a disruptive student to gain a teacher's attention. I wondered what position Anthony would assume or be placed into in his new grade and class. His first-grade teachers, Mrs. Cullen and Mrs. Adams, established a classroom with students in a passive role, in which they were treated as a class rather than as a group of individual students (Dillon, 2000). Each day, all of the students spent 1 hour copying a message from the board, then going to the class library for an hour. Following these activities, the students were divided into two groups, where each teacher worked with one group in reading. In the group, teachers read from the basal text, then students independently completed corresponding worksheets.

Anthony developed complicated positionings during this year

(Harré & Gillett, 1994). He conformed during the copying task and completed it quickly. Often he would start tomorrow's copying task the day before, so he would have more time in the library. (All assignments started the same: "Today is. . . ." "On this day, we will. . . .") While Anthony completed the task, he expended no extra energy on it. He never read the message; he just hurriedly copied it, raised his hand, had his teacher check it for accuracy, and left for the library. During this activity, Anthony assumed a passive position and completed a task he was expected to do. Surprisingly, he was not resistant and did not disrupt this daily task.

Whereas many students might have only a few minutes in the library, Anthony typically had an hour or more each day. The library was where Anthony was happiest, although his teachers often reminded him, "Read. Don't talk to your friends." In a year's worth of observations, Anthony never read in the library. He moved from student to student (just boys) and chatted with them. He always had a book in hand but never opened it. By having a book, he conformed to teachers' expectations. However, he challenged their expectations by never reading. His only joy was in talking to friends while they pretended to read. As I watched him in the library, I thought of him as a *sneaky kid*. On the surface, it appeared that he conformed and was a compliant student, but when I watched closely, it was clear that he subverted all the reading expectations of his teachers.

During small-group reading, Anthony always moved to the back of the group. Groups were large, typically 16 children, so he was not observed. On most days, Anthony continued quiet conversations with his friends while his teacher read. Following reading, he completed worksheets, but never with much enthusiasm. His goal was to be finished, not to learn what was expected on the practice sheet.

Throughout the year, Anthony never formed a relationship with either of his teachers. He passively completed assignments and sought out relationships with his friends. This passive compliance has also been described by Fairclough (1989) and Giroux (1988), when they observed students who fulfilled classroom expectations without engagement. They added to this discussion by suggesting that this type of compliant behavior is engaged in more frequently by students from high-poverty backgrounds who are in less powerful positions in their classroom due to their economic circumstances. Anthony's positioning during this year as passive student and sneaky kid did not serve him well as a literacy learner. He ended first grade below grade level, even though he came in with full phonological awareness and the ability to read predictable text and be conversant in the language of the classroom.

Second Grade

In second grade, Anthony entered a classroom that was workshop oriented, a very different structure than he experienced in kindergarten and first grade. Mrs. Scott and Mrs. Ford expected students to work together as they read and wrote. Both teachers moved in and out of groups to check in and support students' collaboration.

On one of my first visits, the teachers wanted the students to get to know each other better. They organized a scavenger hunt in which the class had to find students who had one brother or sister, liked math, and so on. The teachers reminded students that they could only use a fellow student's name once. Anthony immediately questioned his teachers by asking, "There are 25 blocks on this paper and there are only four students at my table, so how can I only use a student one time?" His teacher replied, "You are right Anthony. How about using the students at your table first, and then we can move around the room." In this example, Anthony negotiated his power relationship with his teacher. Because his teacher was willing to compromise, Anthony and his teacher engaged in collegial positions.

Later in the year, I observed Anthony as he worked with his teacher in a read-aloud with the whole class and in a small reading group. As his teacher read to the class, she often stopped and asked students to talk to a neighbor to predict what might happen next. Anthony loved talking to the boy next to him and volunteering ideas to the whole group about what might happen. In this example, Anthony participated in numerous positions. First, he was a compliant student in that he listened to his teacher read, participated in sharing with another student, and shared with the class. In addition to this position, Anthony also engaged in a somewhat collegial position with his partner, although Anthony's ideas were the only ones shared with the class. Finally, Anthony positioned himself as a smart student as he shared his predictions with the class and made visible his knowledge about text.

Following the read-aloud, students met in small groups with their teachers. In each group, students began by rereading familiar books, then reading a new book. Students took turns orally reading the new book after they completed a picture walk that focused on comprehension. My notes show that when it was Anthony's turn to read, he was ready and read fluently. As he was leaving his group, his teacher shook his hand and said, "It is a pleasure working with you. You are an excellent reader." Anthony smiled as he returned to his desk. In this example, his teacher one again verified Anthony as an excellent reader. She singled him out and conferred this identity on Anthony.

Throughout the year, Anthony participated in this environment, where he shared his ideas with students and his teachers. In this classroom, Anthony regained his identity as an excellent student, achieving grade-level expectations. Even in a small group, his conversations were about books or a text he was writing. He shared his ideas. "I'm writing about a whale," he said, and smiled when his teachers complimented his work.

In second grade, Anthony moved to a unitary position, where he conformed to his teachers' expectations and was singled out as an "excellent reader." As I watched Anthony that year, I realized that he was the person in power. He complied with his teachers because they saw him as smart, and once again, as in kindergarten, he had status in the classroom. In addition, during this year, Anthony separated his identity and positioning of his friends to outside the classroom. Inside the room, he lavished in the "smart kid" position that was connected to his teachers. Outside the classroom, he formed a separate identity in which he was one of the best soccer players, and students sought him out for their team. On the playground, the boys in second and third grade followed his lead in organization of the daily soccer game.

Third Grade

In third grade, Anthony entered a classroom where he only had one teacher, a new experience for him. Anthony's classroom was more structured than it had been in second grade, in that Ms. Read expected students to be on-task and to talk only when she provided time for it. Students rarely worked in small groups where they could chat with each other. Anthony conformed to these expectations on most days. On other days, he wandered the room and quietly talked to three other boys, his closest friends in class and on the soccer field. Anthony's teacher described her relationship with Anthony as "being a love–hate relationship." She loved him when he conformed but was frustrated on days when "he fought her and didn't do any work."

Anthony also spent considerable time in third grade building a personal relationship with Ms. Read. Each morning students used the first 45 minutes writing in their journals about animals, people, and events. After they finished writing, students shared their journals with others at their table for editing. Each student read a journal, marked any mistakes, then passed it to the next student. Following writing and editing, students decided whether they wanted to read their entry to the class. After listening to a journal entry, students commented and pondered questions not answered. The student who had read either answered the questions or replied that he or she did not know. Each day, Ms. Read suggested that students go to the library to find the answers to unanswered questions. Anthony always read his journal, and when students had questions he could not answer, he took on the challenge and found answers on the Internet. He used his recess time to visit the neighboring library to find his answers. When recess was over, he always impatiently waited to share his answer, thus securing his position as the smartest in the class, as recognized by his teacher and fellow students.

Anthony verified his positions in a self-narrative that he wrote during the year.

> *I like to play soccer and football with my friends. I am usually the captain. I like math and I like to read. Reading is something you need to learn or you can't pass school. I like being the best reader. I know a lot.*

This piece continued with a long discussion about how learning to read and books "make you smart and let you get a job." Anthony knew that being smart and a leader in the classroom, and with his

friends, were important to his future success. He used these positionings to end the year above grade level in reading.

Fourth Grade

Anthony entered a fourth-grade class where Mrs. Chew, his teacher,
wanted to be in charge but never developed a managed, classroom
community. She taught to the whole class, expected quiet, and her
students never paid attention. She often told her students, "Creative
minds need quiet." I am not sure that her students heard this mantra,
because her classroom was never quiet. She threatened the students
and punished them, but they were never respectful to her. She frequently lamented that she wanted "to teach in a school where the
kids are smart and their parents care." Although I never heard her
say this directly to her students, her indifference to them certainly
transferred this message.

The students defined the classroom community as being in oppo-
sition to the teacher, and Anthony was a leader. He spent his entire
year wandering the room and talking to friends. On several occasions, his teacher sent him to the principal to get him out of the
room. She said, "He is driving me crazy. He just doesn't care about
learning, and he is disrespectful."

Anthony gained a new position in this classroom; not only was
he oppositional to his teacher, but he was also the leader with the
boys in the room. When he was off-task, so were they, and this was
every day. Starting in October, Anthony was sent to the principal's
office almost daily. The following are some of the comments his
teacher made to him throughout the year:

"This has been a bad day. Think about the grief you caused me.
    Do less talking."
"Do not come to school if you are not going to do your work. I'm
    tired of you being a problem. If you act like this tomorrow,
    you will spend the day with the Vice Principal. Don't act like
    poor little Anthony."
"Stop talking back to me."
"Leave the room and go see the Vice Principal. If anyone else

wants to join Anthony, keep up the good work of being like him."

Although Anthony rarely got through a school day without a reprimand, he was definitely the person in the room with the most power. He rolled his eyes at his teacher, disrupted her teaching, and organized the students in cheating. Students had to place their papers in an organizational folder in the back of the room. Once one student had turned in his or her work, all of the other students quietly and individually went to the folder and copied the answers onto their papers. None of the students invested much energy in work, and the teacher never realized that this cheating was occurring.

Anthony also roamed the room. As I looked through my notes, I found that I repeatedly wrote comments similar to the following:

> "Anthony is roaming the room. He goes to another table and talks to the boys. He stands and talks to them. Then he wanders away and then goes back. He stops at one student's place and talks to him. He goes to the library and glances at the books. He checks the time on his watch. He pushes a child, and she goes back to her desk. He goes to a station and fools around with the materials. He returns to his desk and puts his name on his paper. He looks at his watch and then around the room."

What is interesting is that Anthony finished all of his work. Most of it was copied in class, but he fulfilled the expectation. He also did all of his homework. Although he never listened when his teacher taught, he enjoyed silent reading. He read novels like *Charlotte's Web* and many informational texts throughout the year.

At the end of the year, I interviewed Anthony about his year, and he was very positive. Anthony commented that he enjoyed learning about plants and writing reports like the one he did on Bo Jackson. When I probed more, he said that he read on the Internet each night, looking for information, and that he read all the books his grandma gave to him.

Describing Anthony's behavior during this year is complicated. He held the power position in the class, even when he was forced to leave the room. He never left the room quietly; he always left with a demonstration—such as throwing a paper down or glaring at his teacher. Being out of the room on most days, and watching the time and roaming the classroom, were not what I considered a curriculum in which a student would achieve. However, Anthony ended the year above grade level, yet he only participated in a few activities. I was perplexed by this result.

Although I have no clear answers to explain his above-grade-level achievement, there are several possible explanations: (1) Anthony did well because he came to fourth grade as a strong reader and writer, and his independent reading was sufficient to maintain this status; (2) his reading on the Internet and at home provided the practice he needed to continue as a successful reader; or (3) he achieved out of spite, so that his teacher was forced to see him as a smart kid. Resistance toward his teacher and her curriculum provided the impetus for Anthony to achieve.

Fifth Grade

In fifth grade, Anthony faced a unique structure for learning. All of his fifth-grade teachers worked with all of the fifth graders rather than just their homeroom of students. These teachers had presented a plan to their principal, in which they guaranteed that students' movement from class to class would be seamless, and that they would all use the same discipline system, so that there were no behavioral adjustments for students from classroom to classroom.

Every afternoon, each teacher worked with students in reading; students were grouped by informal assessment. In these groups, they read in book clubs and wrote about their reading in journals. Throughout the day, each teacher taught one major subject area to all of the fifth graders: Mrs. Katen taught math; Mr. Bussoni taught social studies; and Mrs. Callep taught science. In addition, each teacher taught spelling and writing and provided AR time on a daily basis.

Anthony was assigned to the homeroom of Mrs. Katen, who was in her second year of teaching and appreciated working with the other fifth-grade teachers who were more experienced. Although I knew Anthony's assigned homeroom, it would have been difficult to discover this after the first few minutes of school. Students moved among the classrooms and interacted with all of the teachers each day. Whenever I asked about a student, all of the teachers came together to provide a description. For example, when I asked about Anthony in September, his teachers replied:

> "He is doing OK. He said he was reading sixth-grade books last year. He wants to be in the highest group. We are going to try him out in the fifth-grade reading club (the middle group) and see how he does. He wants to do well. He has high expectations for himself."

This description of Anthony is very different from the one held by his fourth-grade teacher. It supports the observations of McCarthey (2002) that identity is fluid and, for students, is dependent on their classroom environments and the relationships they establish with their teachers.

The atmosphere in all of the classrooms was that of a workshop. Although there was some direct instruction, most instruction occurred in small group, where there was much discussion. In reading, all of the students participated in book clubs, where they chose the book they would read from a selection offered by the teacher. (On most occasions, these books were organized by theme—explorers, for instance.) In addition to book clubs, students participated in AR every day, where they independently read books and took quizzes.

I wondered how Anthony would position himself in this complicated structure, with three teachers and numerous configurations of students. Early on, Anthony recognized that this year was unique and a supportive environment for him. In September, Anthony wrote a journal entry that demonstrated this realization:

> *This school year I will try hard in class and be a good student. I will turn in all my work. I will not get in trouble as much as last year. I will be the best I could be this year. I am going to do good this year. I like fifth grade better then all the grades I have been to. My teachers are nice. I have a lot of friends in fifth grade. We get to talk about what we read. . . .*

Throughout the year, I observed Anthony engage in learning with his teachers and his classmates. Frequently his conversations with his teachers matched the oral challenges his teachers offered the class. For example, one day, students were discussing the planets, in particular, Neptune. Anthony said that in the illustration, "the dark spots are storms and one is as big as the earth." Mrs. Katen replied, "I am not sure." Anthony answered, "Then prove it. See if I am right." Whereas some teachers might see this as disrespectful, the fifth-grade teachers constantly challenged their students to find proof for their statements, and students often expected the same of their teachers. The result was that Anthony and Mrs. Katen searched the Internet together to get clarification and then shared their search with the class.

By January, Anthony moved into the highest book club and was considered above grade level in reading. As I observed his book club reading *Oh, Brother* (Wilson, 1988), I noted the relationships between the students and their teacher. Throughout this book club, Mr. Bussoni never moved into a position as the most knowledgeable of readers. He participated as an interested reader, and all members of this group participated as colleagues. One student queried, "Do you think Andrew is in a gang?" Following this question, the students and the teacher reread the text to see whether they could decide. Anthony offered, "He is dirty." Other students found other pieces of text, but the question was never resolved. Then Eric said, "This book is about his family." This trigger statement resulted in a long discussion about the family in the book and students' personal families. As the conversation continued, Mr. Bussoni quietly left the group to join another.

In addition to book clubs, I observed that these teachers never left their classrooms. They opened their doors to students before school, during recess, and after school. On some occasions, students came in to complete work. However, on most occasions, students came in to chat with their teachers about out-of-school events. In fact, sixth-grade students often returned to chat with their fifth-grade teachers. Frequently, Anthony abandoned soccer to visit Mr. Bussoni's class during recess. When I observed him during these unofficial school times, he often read books for AR, so that he would meet or exceed his goal. Anthony never had a problem meeting these goals, so I once again saw how important building a personal relationship with teachers was for Anthony.

Unlike his behavior in other grades, Anthony was never defiant or resistant in fifth grade. When his teachers organized their classrooms as learning communities, Anthony readily participated as a member. Additionally, he served in leadership positions conferred by his teachers, such as tutoring a student or taking lunch count to the office. What is unique about his positioning in fifth grade is that Anthony was not singled out for a special relationship with his teacher, as had happened in kindergarten; rather, all students were treated as individuals within a large learning community. I believe that because all students were valued as individuals, Anthony had no reason to be resistant, as he had been when students were treated as a group.

At the end of the year, both his teachers and Anthony reflected on the year. His teachers noted, "Anthony challenges himself to be the best. He works hard. He wants relationships with his teachers, and he seeks recognition." Anthony commented, "Fifth grade is cool. I'm second in reading. I am a good reader because I read a lot. I loved this year."

Sixth Grade

In sixth grade, Anthony entered Ms. Jones's classroom, although students moved between her classroom and that of Mr. McGuire for instruction. The only difference from fifth grade was that Mr. McGuire worked with all students for reading, and Ms. Jones taught math.

Anthony moved back to multiple positions during that year. With Ms. Jones, he often was resistant. She described him: "He is like the weather. He is either motivated or cranky." When Ms. Jones worked with students, she most often assumed an authoritative position, and students were expected to comply. On some days, Anthony conformed; on others, he resisted.

However, Mr. McGuire adopted a workshop environment for reading instruction. In this environment, Anthony, once again, was a colleague. Anthony wrote about one experience working with a group:

I liked what we did. It was fun. Our group worked good but we had some problems. We messed up a couple of times but we solved it.

Clearly, Anthony was happiest when collegial positions were assumed in his classrooms. During these times, Anthony was a motivated student. When he was expected to comply without a voice, Anthony often resisted, particularly if he was treated as one of a group of students rather than an individual.

Summary

Anthony's classroom communities and the positions taken by his teachers clearly resulted in Anthony reframing his identities. These identities and resulting positions determined who he was as a literacy learner throughout his school experiences. When he could build a personal relationship with his teachers and they saw him as smart, he developed a "school kid" identity (Flores-Gonzalez, 2002), irrespective of his relationships with other students. For Anthony, school was all about the relationship he had with his teachers—and he valued collegial relationships most. Anthony also had an identity with his friends. When he did not perceive that he was valued by his teachers and was placed in a subservient position, he inappropriately interacted with his friends in the classroom. And Anthony was always the leader among his friends, because he was smart and very good at sports. When he was valued as an individual by his teacher, he interacted with friends in appropriate ways inside and outside the classroom.

This view enriches the description of Anthony as a literacy learner. Anthony constructed how he would behave and learn in each of his classroom situations. At the end of sixth grade, each teacher had a different perspective on Anthony. Some saw him as nothing but trouble, and others viewed him as a contributing and positive member of the class. Anthony's position and the position in which he placed his teachers had little to do with his learning. The most vivid example of this was his fourth-grade experience, in which Anthony maintained an above-grade-level performance in reading and was oppositional to his teacher the entire year. However, school took on new meaning for Anthony when he participated in collegial relationships with his teachers and other students. In these equitable power relationships, he deepened his understanding of literacy, in general, and of the books he was reading and the texts he was writing in particular.

RESILIENCE THEORY PERSPECTIVE

One of the most important and consistent findings in resilience research is the power of schools, especially of teachers, to turn a child's life from risk to resilience.
—BONNIE BENARD (2004, p. 65)

Similar to positioning theory, the concept of resilience is new to most educators. When I wrote about children prenatally exposed to crack/ cocaine in 1999, reviewers found the topic of resilience troublesome. They were not sure how this informed my study about the literacy development of these children. However, I discovered that resilience had much to add to the description of these young children, and without it, there was no way to appreciate these children's extraordinary accomplishments (Barone, 1999).

In 2005, the subject of resilience and its connection to student success has moved from solely academic writing to popular magazines. In a recent issue of *Time* magazine, Gorman (2005) discussed resilience and how it explains why some children succeed in school and others from similar circumstances do not. She reported that the parental bond is the most critical factor for resilience, but other factors, such as talent, finding a champion, and looking within, build resilience.

Similarly, Waxman, Gray, and Padrón (2004a) note that resilience helps to explain why some high-poverty students do well in school, whereas others struggle. Moriarty (1987) describes a resilient child as one who "is oriented toward the future, is living ahead, with hope" (p. 106). Resilience, like identity or positioning, is fluid. At times, students may have more resilience than at other times in their lives. For example, a student may be achieving in school, but when his or her mother and father are divorced, this student struggles.

Certainly students come to school with more or less resilience; nevertheless, schools and teachers can nurture resilience. Waxman, Gray, and Padrón (2004b) reported that Minneapolis Public Schools developed resilience policies that center around five strategies:

1. Offer opportunities for students to develop personal relationships with teachers.
2. Increase students' sense of mastery in their lives.
3. Build social competencies as well as academic skills.
4. Reduce the stressors that students do not need to face.
5. Generate school and community resources to support the needs of students. (p. 52)

Minneapolis Public School personnel see these strategies as critical to closing the achievement gap.

Moving from schools to teachers, Benard (1997) identified the characteristics of teachers considered to be *turnaround teachers*. She noted that these teachers modeled three essential dimensions of resilience. The first involves caring and establishing relationships between students and adults. The second is centered in opportunities to participate and contribute, and the third is about setting high expectations. Benard further described these teachers as persons who do not judge students but understand that they are doing the best they can. Turnaround teachers build on the strengths of students, are student-centered, and motivate their students.

As I observed at Howard, I noted that several teachers did more than teach the curriculum. They found time before, during, and after school to chat, work with students, and as a result build friendships. During class time, they nurtured students as they helped them achieve the high expectations they set. These teachers understood that students at Howard came from high-poverty situations, and that many lived with a single parent or foster parents in neighborhoods populated by gangs. They relied on their school and church to support them and provide safe places to learn and grow. However, these teachers did not define their students by the circumstances into which they were born. Rather, they valued their students as individuals and had hope and high expectations for their futures.

I chose several examples that describe teachers—*turnaround teachers*—modeling and supporting students in developing resilience. Four teachers stood out when I reanalyzed the data. These teachers developed personal relationships with students and supported them as they attempted to reach high expectations. The first teacher, Mrs. Stevens, a second-grade teacher, constantly supported her ELL students in learning English. The second teacher, Mrs. Spears, continuously shared messages with her whole class and with individual students about how smart they were and how they could achieve anything. The last two teachers are fifth-grade teachers: Mrs. Callep bought books for students to read at home when she discovered their favorite authors, and Mr. Bussoni always found time to have personal conversations with students. I found it interesting that most of the examples come from intermediate teachers rather than primary teachers. It seemed that at Howard, the intermediate teachers, even though their classes were larger than primary classes, found time to converse with students and support them as individuals in their academic and personal endeavors.

Mrs. Stevens's Second-Grade Classroom

Mrs. Stevens was the first teacher that I noticed constantly making positive comments to students and recognizing students for in-class and out-of-class behavior. The following are some of the routine comments she made to students as she worked with them:

> "Mistakes are not bad. We learn from them."
> "Soon you will be able to read this all by yourself. You won't need my help."
> "It is fun to go to college. I know you will all go."
> "I learned English in high school. I am impressed with how much you know about English and how you spell so many words. You know more than I did, and I went to college."

[as children completed a Venn diagram about alligators and croc-
odiles:] "I didn't know that. You are so smart. I learn from
you every day."

[talking to Fredy:] "It is so good to see you growing up and becoming responsible. Aren't you proud?"

These comments permeated the classroom. Each day, students heard
positive comments, most often directed to them personally, that nurtured expectations of doing well academically and striving to attend
college.

In addition to these comments, Mrs. Stevens regularly acknowledged the strengths of students in learning English. Because she also
learned English as a new language, she was aware of the struggles in
acquiring academic English. For example, she encouraged her students to use a word from their home language when writing. She
said, "Just write the word you know. Don't worry about the language. We can always change it to English. Just write what is important to you." In this way, students moved beyond safe words and
topics and began to write meaningful journal entries and stories that
matched their thinking.

Finally, Mrs. Stevens was very aware of the out-of-school lives of
her students. She often went to programs or baseball games to watch
them. One day, I heard her tell Julio, "You are one of the best climb-
ers. I saw you at the top of the monkey bars." Julio smiled at this.
Mrs. Stevens was the first teacher that I observed who was aware of
her students' lives outside of the classroom and routinely shared this
information in the classroom.

Mrs. Spears's Fourth-Grade Classroom

Similar to Mrs. Stevens, Mrs. Spears believed in the academic and
personal strengths of her students, and frequently conveyed these
messages to her students. She often stopped instruction and complimented students, and she also quietly talked to individual students
about an accomplishment. The following are some of these comments:

"I know you will do quality work, because you are talented students."

[to a student:] "Your work is awesome. I get chills just reading it."

[as a student talked to her about his dad:] "I love to hear about your family. I know they love you and take good care of you."

"Mario, I saw you play soccer. You are good at kicking. Maritza, I heard you play the piano and sing. You have a beautiful voice. Calvin, you know so many words. You are a word expert."

And also like Mrs. Stevens, Mrs. Spears found time to go to students' out-of-school activities. She said, "During these activities, I get to chat with their parents, and we get to know each other. I tell them the good things about their child, and then I ask them to help me. They always make sure that their child reads and writes at home. That is why they are so successful in class."

In a conversation at the end of the year, Mrs. Spears described her students and her goals for them:

"I think they're great. They do have drive, and I think it's important to me and to them. I just let them know how important it is to get an education and do their best. I just tell them, 'Do the best you can. It's important.' We've kind of got out of the mode of being dishwashers and maids. At the beginning of the year, they want to clean houses, like my mother cleaned houses. And I go, 'You know, there's nothing wrong with that.' We just rehash things a lot and I go, 'You know, you're really, really smart, and I bet your mom and dad want you to go to college.' And as the year progresses, they really want to accomplish more, even if they have a little goal, you know. This year has been good. They've worked really hard, they focused, and they did the best they could."

This quote demonstrated the confidence that Mrs. Spears had in her students. She saw the strengths rather than the deficits or home backgrounds of her students. Throughout the year, she posed goals and challenges for her students, and they always achieved them: Some of these challenges were completed in class, such as higher grades or reading longer, more complicated books; others were challenges outside of class, such as considering college or playing a sport rather than watching television.

Mrs. Callep's and Mr. Bussoni's Fifth-Grade Classrooms

Similar to Mrs. Stevens and Mrs. Spears, Mr. Bussoni and Mrs. Callep supported students. What I found unique to these two teachers was the way they supported students in either class. During recess, for example, students felt comfortable visiting either teacher. Whereas in some classes, coming in to the classroom was a punishment, students elected to spend this time with their teachers, even if it meant not playing soccer or football during recess.

These teachers also tailored comments to support students in reading and writing. For example, they knew the book preferences of their students. Mrs. Callep realized that Eric loved books by Gary Paulsen; she bought him all of the Paulsen books, so he could enjoy them in school and at home. She made a gift of these books to Eric, and he was amazed and pleased that they were his to keep. He said, "I love Paulsen and my teacher bought all of his books. I don't know which book to start with."

As part of their literacy curriculum, these teachers had their students write about themselves as readers and writers. They used these jottings to note differences in the way students perceived themselves. The following is one of these entries written by Josie:

> When I was in the first grade I hated to read because I didn't know how. Now I love to read because we go to the library and check out tons of books. Our teachers talked to the librarian so we have more choices of books. When I read I feel like I'm there. It's really fun to read and I get excited when I read. . . .

This response gives evidence of the quality of reading in which these students were engaged. It demonstrates that these teachers were willing to negotiate the library rules, so that students had multiple books to read and explore.

During the year, Mrs. Callep explained to me why the fifth-grade students got along so well. I had not noticed any discipline concerns and wondered why. She said:

> "They understand each other. When a child is having a bad day, other kids move in to help. These kids have a lot of resilience, you know, perseverance, they have an 'I can do it' attitude."

I was surprised to hear the word *resilience* in her description. Clearly, Mrs. Callep and Mr. Bussoni helped develop this resilience in their students.

Although most of this section has focused on how teachers supported resilience in students, students were also resilient in the way they managed their at-home and at-school lives. For example, several of the focal students had brothers and sisters who were in gangs, yet they resisted. Other focal students had parents in gangs, and they found ways to exist in these homes without joining in gang activity. Several focal students had parents who were incarcerated during the study, and despite this trauma, they did well in school. One student saw his mother placed in a facility to deal with alcohol abuse; although he had numerous home changes during this time, he continued to do well in school. Finally, several students experienced their parents' divorce, remarriage, having children, and divorcing once again.

These experiences certainly were challenges to these students. However, what is powerful is that they rebounded from these challenges and succeeded in school. Without the support of caring teachers, they may not have been able to negotiate their school curriculum while they survived these stressful situations at home.

FINAL THOUGHTS

The strength of pursuing multiple views of students' achievement is that it moves away from simple, single explanations of literacy learning. Certainly teachers' instruction provided support for literacy development. However, conversational communities, collaborative positionings, and turnaround teachers supported students in their literacy accomplishments. Moreover, these views into classroom learning demonstrate the nonstatic view of students as literacy learners. Certainly, Anthony highlights the changeability of literacy identities and their relationship to learning.

I also believe that when we consider these alternative views of literacy, the professionalism of teachers is evident. This chapter has highlighted teachers who continued to teach writing process even when this was not measured directly in test scores, supported collaborative learning even when this was not directly measured in test scores, valued a child's home language even when this was not directly measured in test scores, and built personal relationships with students even when this was not directly measured in test scores. They understood that teaching was about supporting individual students academically and emotionally, inside and outside of school. Teaching was about the friendships developed with students and their parents.

REFERENCES

Almasi, J. (2002). Research-based comprehension practices that create higher-level discussions. In C. Block, L. Gambrell, & M. Pressley (Eds.), *Improving comprehension instruction* (pp. 229–242). San Francisco: Jossey-Bass.

Barone, D. (1999). *Resilient children: Stories of poverty, drug exposure, and literacy development.* Newark, DE: International Reading Association.

Benard, B. (1997). *Turning it around for all youth: From risk to resilience* (ERIC/CUE Digest No. 126). New York: ERIC Clearinghouse on Urban Education.

Benard, B. (2004). *Resiliency: What we have learned.* San Francisco: WestEd.

Dillon, D. (2000). *Reconsidering how to meet the literacy needs of all students.* Newark, DE: International Reading Association.

Dressman, M. (1997). *Literacy in the library: Negotiating the spaces between order and desire.* Westport, CT: Bergin & Garvey.

Dyson, A. (1993). *Social worlds of children learning to write in an urban primary school.* New York: Teachers College Press.

Dyson, A. (2003). *The brothers and sisters learn to write.* New York: Teachers College Press.

Enciso, P. (1996). Why engagement in reading matters to Molly. *Reading and Writing Quarterly: Overcoming Learning Difficulties, 12,* 171–194.

Evans, K. (1996). Creating spaces for equity?: The role of positioning in peer-led literature discussions. *Language Arts, 73,* 194–203.

Fairclough, N. (1989). *Language and power.* London: Longman.

Flores-Gonzalez, N. (2002). *School kids/street kids: Identity development in Latino students.* New York: Teachers College Press.

Foley, D. (1990). *Learning capitalist culture: Deep in the heart of Texas.* Philadelphia: University of Pennsylvania Press.

Gee, J. (2001). Reading as situated language: A sociolinguistic perspective. *Journal of Adolescent and Adult Literacy, 44,* 714–725.

Giroux, H. (1988). *Schooling and the struggle for public life.* Minneapolis: University of Minnesota Press.

Gorman, C. (2005, February 17). The importance of resilience. *Time.* Available online at www.time.com/time/2005/happiness/the_importance_of_resil20_print.html.

Harré, R., & Gillett, G. (1994). *The discursive mind.* Thousand Oaks, CA: Sage.

Harré, R., & Langenhove, L. (Eds.). (1999). *Positioning theory.* Oxford, UK: Blackwell.

McCarthey, S. (2002). *Students' identities and literacy learning.* Newark, DE: International Reading Association.

Moriarty, A. (1987). John, a boy who acquired resilience. In E. J. Anthony & B. J. Cohler (Eds.), *The invulnerable child* (pp. 106–144). New York: Guilford Press.

Nieto, S. (2002). *Language, culture, and teaching.* Mahwah, NJ: Erlbaum.

Paulsen, G. (1987). *Hatchet.* New York: Simon & Schuster.

Purcell-Gates, V., McIntyre, E., & Freppon, P. (1995). Learning written storybook language in school: A comparison of low-SES children in skills-based and whole language classrooms. *American Educational Research Journal, 32,* 659–685.

Sloan, G. (1991). *The child as critic: Teaching literature in elementary and middle schools.* New York: Teachers College Press.

Waxman, H., Gray, J., & Padrón, Y. (2004a). Introduction and overview. In H. Waxman, Y. Padrón, & J. Gray (Eds.), *Educational resiliency: Student, teacher, and school perspectives* (pp. 3–10). Greenwich, CT: Information Age.

Waxman, H., Gray, J., & Padrón, Y. (2004b). Promoting educational resilience for student at-risk of failure. In H. Waxman, Y. Padrón, & J. Gray (Eds.), *Educational resiliency: Student, teacher, and school perspectives* (pp. 37–62). Greenwich, CT: Information Age.

Wilkinson, L., & Silliman, E. (2000). Classroom language and literacy learning. In M. Kamil, P. Mosenthal, P. D. Pearson, & R. Barr (Eds.), *Handbook of reading research* (Vol. III, pp. 337–360). Mahwah, NJ: Erlbaum.

Willis, P. (1977). *Learning to labor: How working class kids get working class jobs.* New York: Columbia University Press.

Wilson, J. (1988). *Oh, brother.* New York: Scholastic.

Wolf, S. (2004). *Interpreting literature with children.* Mahwah, NJ: Erlbaum.

Chapter 5

Conundrums and Discoveries Along the Way

A teacher's beliefs about learners and the learning process can create tensions and problems that affect how a teacher works to support learners' needs.
—DEBORAH R. DILLON (2000, p. 80)

As I studied students' learning and instruction for 7 years, I identified interesting conundrums along the way. At times I noticed that teachers highlighted issues such as high-stakes testing and balancing test preparation with teaching students. At other times, I made these discoveries at the end of the study, when I spent a lengthy time with the data; for example, in this way, I identified an issue centered on curriculum alignment.

I begin this chapter by exploring these conundrums and end with a view into the classrooms of two exemplary teachers. One of these teachers has given me much to reflect upon since I first visited her. Mrs. Spears taught to her whole class and did not provide instruction targeted to individual students, yet her students achieved. Mr. Bussoni, another exemplary teacher, worked with his whole class but also provided individual instruction to students. These teachers were so very different in their instructional approach, yet they made a difference to students' achievement and beliefs. I wondered why. Finally, I highlight several of the major discoveries of this study. These discoveries, in particular, can be used as discussion and study points in schools serving students from high-poverty backgrounds.

CONUNDRUMS

High-Stakes Testing and Teaching

From the beginning until the end of this study, the principals and teachers at Howard Elementary worried about how students would do on standardized assessments and what would happen if scores did not improve. School scores were made public in the newspaper, and the state organized schools and labeled them based on achievement scores. If a school failed to perform on achievement tests and stayed in the *needs improvement* category, there were expectations that the state would take over the school. Often I heard teachers say, "They can take this school over. I want to see how they help these kids." At one point in my study, the state organized a team to help improve scores and student learning at Howard. This committee, and others assigned to the school to enhance achievement, often mandated programs that teachers had to implement. For example, when the focal students were in fourth grade, each teacher was required to spend about 30 minutes each day on a math facts program. This program continued until the end of my study. One teacher commented, "Only in a school like this would something like this happen. Now I lose a half-hour every day to basic facts. When will my kids learn math?"

In literacy, the school used Comprehensive Early Literacy Learning/Extended Literacy Learning (CELL/ExLL) for professional development. Throughout my time at the school, teachers were free to implement the best strategies they learned. They also had literacy specialists to help. Additionally, the school adopted the AR program to enhance reading achievement and students' facility with test questions. As my study progressed, I saw more and more time given to AR (see more discussion of this later in the chapter). However, overall, teachers had extensive freedom to design and manage their literacy curricula. I believe that teachers maintained their freedom for instruction because Howard came off of the state *needs improvement* list. Had this not happened, I believe a more prescriptive literacy program would have been mandated.

The most direct change in instruction based on testing was the focus in writing. Most of intermediate students' writing was to prepare for the state test. This writing included from one to three paragraphs about an assigned topic. Students then learned to evaluate this writing based on the writing traits of organization, voice, ideas, and conventions. Of the focal students who took the writing test in fourth and sixth grade, five improved their scores in sixth grade where expectations were more sophisticated than in fourth grade (see Table 2.1). Moving beyond the focal students to the school as a whole, fourth graders at Howard typically struggled with the state writing test. Table 5.1 shows the writing scores for 4 years. These scores were all below district averages. Looking at the table it is clear that there was much volatility around the scores. School scores were improving until 2002, when scores dropped across all categories. The category with the largest drop was voice. I wondered if students were finding it difficult to bring voice into assessment writing when so much attention was given to organization and conventions.

In 2003, the state reporting process for the writing test changed. The state now reported percentages of students who were developing, approaching, meeting, or exceeding the expectations of the writing assessment (see Table 5.2). For this year, the results for fourth graders at Howard were developing, 24.7%; approaching, 47.2%; meeting, 25.8%; and exceeding, 2.2%. For the first two categories, these percentages were above the district and state results; thus, Howard had more students scoring in developing and approaching categories, not a positive result. In the meeting and exceeding catego-

TABLE 5.1. Writing Test Score Results

| Year | Percentage of proficient students in four areas | | | | Percentage of students scoring 3 or higher on . . . | |
	Ideas and content	Organization	Voice	Conventions	All four traits	One or more traits
2002	27.5	26.4	24.2	36.3	16.5	48.4
2001	31.4	31.45	40	47.1	20	61.4
2000	21.2	25.8	25.8	42.4	10.6	54.5
1999	36.4	22.7	27.3	29.5	9.1	56.8

TABLE 5.2. District and State Writing Scores: 2003

Developing expectations			Approaching expectations			Meeting expectations			Exceeding expectations		
School	District	State	School	District	State	School	District	State	School	District	State
24.7	18.4	22.4	47.2	22.2	24.1	25.8	33.3	33.2	2.2	26.1	20.4

ries, Howard had more students scoring below the district and state results.

Most likely, even with the dips in improvement in 2002, writing test improvement occurred because of the extensive test practice that students experienced in school. I wondered about how this test practice affected the more general writing experiences of students. Typically, we expect that students write to their own topics, to the topics of teachers guided by curriculum, in response to learning, and so on, in their classrooms. This writing has multiple audiences, including self, teachers, parents, and others. However, at Howard, and I am sure at other elementary schools, writing instruction, in fourth grade in particular, narrowed to writing to an anonymous assessor. This narrow view of writing influenced what students and teachers considered for writing instruction and learning at Howard. I wondered, with limited writing experiences, how do students understand writing, and the power of writing, when the majority of writing is three-paragraph essays written to predetermined topics? Would students have done better on the state tests if they had richer writing experiences? These questions are still puzzles to be considered at the end of the study.

Additionally, there was a more subtle change in the school's climate—constant stress about testing, or the results of testing. Although this stress occurs in all schools, it is most visible in high-poverty schools where threats of state takeovers are more prevalent. The research of Calkins, Montgomery, Santman, and Falk (1998) documented that teachers are conflicted in preparing for tests and meeting the expectations of their curriculum. Teachers want their students to do well, but they are frustrated with the time necessary to prepare students adequately for assessment (Smith, 1991). Hoffman,

Assaf, and Paris (2001) also found that teachers are frustrated with test preparation when they do not view it as supporting students' literacy development. Teachers like Mrs. Erin, as seen in Chapter 4, continuously scrutinized their curriculum and how it supported test scores. They worried about direct benefits from teaching to testing. As a result, students experienced more worksheets that were similar to state tests. And although teachers increased test preparation time, they worried about it, and how it diminished time for teaching. Importantly, this stress was evident before No Child Left Behind legislation.

Relationships with Parents Who Do Not Speak English

At Howard, the majority of parents did not speak English fluently, particularly mothers, who most often stayed at home with their children. This school reached out to parents by creating a parent center that had social workers and others who supported parents' basic needs. They also had interpreters available to help parents with school and other communication. So there were resources on the school campus to help parents, particularly to help them negotiate the school's expectations. However, I observed few parents involved with teachers other than during conference time or at a school program.

When students were in kindergarten, their parents walked them to school and returned to pick them up each day. Once students entered kindergarten, this group of parents often stood outside the classrooms and chatted. Although these parents were visible on campus, they were infrequently invited into classrooms. During my time observing in kindergarten, only one parent ever came in to help with instruction. Eric's mother often helped in the room by preparing materials or supervising class parties. The only time that parents were invited in was typically during parent conferences twice each year.

Although teachers did not encourage parent involvement in their classrooms, the principal had monthly meetings for parents. He established morning meetings for parents to chat with him about school in general, or about their children. There was usually a good turnout for these morning meetings. There was also a large turnout for parent conferences. In my time at Howard, this was always about 90% of parents. So parents were able and willing to be involved with school.

The conundrum is that whereas teachers infrequently invited parents into their classrooms, they lamented the lack of parental involvement. One teacher said, "I know these kids would do better if their parents cared. They never are involved with school." Another teacher complained, "They can't even help them with homework, because they don't speak English. They don't try."

However, when I talked to parents and to my focal students, I found these teachers' comments to be inaccurate. Of the focal students, only Maritza's parents did not read or write with her. They explained to me, "The school will teach her to read and write." All of the other focal students' parents read and wrote with their children routinely. For example, Jaryd said, "My mom helps me write." Heidee informed me, "I want to read like my Dad. He reads to me every night." And Maria said, "My Dad reads to me in Spanish and English. I play school with my brother. That's how I learned to read." Clearly, these parents were involved with reading and writing, and saw the connections between reading at home and successful reading achievement in school.

I wondered if teachers maintained these beliefs, for they found it difficult to communicate with parents; therefore, parents were not invited into classrooms. Because there was distance between the parents and teachers, and because teachers struggled with communication, these myths continued. When I asked, one teacher said, "Yes it's hard. I need a translator to help us communicate." Another teacher said, "Instruction is in English, and they can't help." As a result, language served as a barrier for partnerships and understandings between teachers and parents.

Because most parents were not conversant in English and teachers were not fluent in parents' home languages, many teachers marginalized parents. They found it difficult to communicate with parents, and they minimized shared events to only those involving problematic behaviors or to district scheduled events such as parent conferences, even when there were interpreters available on the school campus. The reciprocal of this action was that teachers then saw parents as not being involved with school or their children's learning. This belief limited any possible relationships with parents, and parents were never integral to the school or to their children's achievement. And for some teachers this belief/misconception limited the expectations they had for students. For example, one teacher said, "Parents don't care, so these kids have no hope of doing well here or in the future."

What Is Grade-Level Achievement?

As a way of determining the achievement of the focal children, I periodically asked each teacher if a particular focal child was at, above, or below grade level in reading. I believed that with the pressure of having children meet grade-level expectations, teachers would easily be able to provide this information about the focal students. For some teachers, this was an easy question, and they used assessment data to answer. For example in second grade, Eric's teacher established that he was above grade level, because "he reads independently at level 24. He is in the top reading group and we are working on comprehension. His DRA [Developmental Reading Assessment] has him decoding at fourth grade, but his comprehension is not there yet." However, other teachers pondered this question and described literacy behaviors but did not comment on assessments in making these determinations. For example, in fifth grade, Jaryd's teacher described him as below grade level, because "it depends on interest level. I would say his independent reading level is like maybe third grade. His comprehension is near fourth or fifth grade." These were hunches she had, and although descriptive and maybe accurate, she did not use any assessment data to support her decisions.

Teachers at Howard established a school protocol of informal assessments that the literacy specialists anticipated would guide instruction. There was a calendar when assessments were given, and results were provided to the literacy specialists so that a school and classroom view could be shared. Results were frequently used for in-class and additional support instruction for struggling students. A list of the required informal assessments follows:

Schoolwide assessments

- Scholastic Reading Inventory (SRI; four times per year) (for more details, see teacher.scholastic.com/sri/)
- Phonological Awareness Literacy Screening (PALS; twice per year) (for more details, see pals.virginia.edu)

Primary classes

- Observation survey (ongoing)
- Letter Identification Test (twice per year)
- Writing Vocabulary Test (twice per year)
  —Students were expected to write all the words they knew in a specified amount of time.
- Concepts about Print Test (twice per year)
- Word Knowledge Test (twice per year)
  —Developmental Spelling Inventory
- Dictation (twice per year)
- Developmental Reading Assessments (three times per year)

Intermediate grades

- John's Reading Inventory (three times per year)
- Writing Sample (twice per year)
- Writing Vocabulary Test (twice per year)
- STAR Reading Renaissance Place (STAR) Reading Assessment (three times per year)
- Accelerated Reader (ongoing)

ELLs

- Language Assessment Scales (LAS) testing (five times per year)

In addition to informal assessment, there was formal assessment. Students took the state criterion-referenced tests (CRTs) in third grade and Terra Nova exams in fourth grade (later changed to Iowa Test of Basic Skills [ITBS]). Additionally, students in fourth and sixth grade took the state writing assessments. The school district also had a CRT testing program for students. Importantly, this huge amount of assessment was in place before No Child Left Behind legislation was enacted.

Several issues were connected to assessment. I believe that one of the issues with this repertoire of assessments is that students did not have consistent results across all measures. Teachers and literacy specialists were concerned about this and began a study to better understand discrepancies. An example is Sandra's test results in second grade. In August, Sandra's running record placed her as a midyear first grader and the STAR test was consistent with a first-grade midyear placement. At the end of second grade, Sandra was reading level 27 material, an equivalent for fifth grade (see Table 2.1), and her STAR test placed her at the end of second grade. The assessments varied, with Sandra being either above or at grade level. Teachers wondered which assessment was most valid with these variable results.

A second issue is that teachers valued different measures to determine students' grade level placement or did not use the measures at all. In primary grades, teachers typically relied on running records and the grade-level books students read. Other informal assessments were collected but did not result in grade-level decisions. However, a focus on leveled text and running records ended in the intermediate grades, where teachers relied more on AR assessment results. Students also became aware of grade-level placement in intermediate grades because of the books they could choose to read for AR time. For example, Maritza decided she was doing "real bad" in reading in fifth grade, because "I only have 48% on my AR goal. I need to pick easy books to reach my goal. I want to read fifth grade books, but I don't do well on the tests." She knew that to be considered a good reader, she had to achieve her AR goal during each report card period.

A third issue is that, for some teachers, the informal assessments were just filed away. They taught the whole class as though students were all the same. In fourth grade, for example, Mrs. Chew struggled in finding time in her day for these required assessments. She was still trying to complete beginning-of-the-year assessments in January. Although this was problematic for the literacy consultants, Mrs. Chew only saw that the informal assessments were interfering with instructional time. She did not group students, and her expectation was that all students would complete the same assignments with the same results. For her, informal assessment was just a chore to be completed, so that the literacy specialist could check her off as being done.

A fourth issue was that teachers only used norm-referenced tests for school data: Teachers did not consider these formal assessments for grade-level determinations. As I noted in previous chapters, a child could score higher on a CRT test and still be considered a poorer reader than another child who also scored higher. These tests were only seen as measures of school achievement and did not seem very influential in classrooms, other than when curricular instruction was geared to test preparation.

I found the conundrum centered on grade-level achievement particularly interesting. Today, when all schools are expected to have all students meet grade-level expectations by third grade, I ponder how grade level might be determined. With No Child Left Behind legislation, all states have determined a formal criterion approved by the federal government to decide whether grade level is achieved in third grade. And in most states, this criterion gets more difficult every other year. For instance, the percentage of children in third grade who meet the grade-level goal increases, so in one state, in 2003, only 26% of students needed to be at grade level in third grade, as measured by the state CRT, but in 2005, 39% must meet this goal to achieve adequate yearly progress (AYP). Although this is a set criterion in one grade level to determine grade-level achievement, most teachers, based on this study, use other criteria for this decision. The issue of grade level is one that teachers, schools, and districts will need to explore, particularly if they expect to meet the needs of struggling and accelerated readers.

Vertical and Horizontal Curriculum Alignment

I noted over the years of observation at Howard that there was no consistency in literacy curricula within a grade or across grades. Even with systematic professional development in place, there were great variations in curriculum. This was not surprising given that teachers were free to bring back to their classrooms the preferred strategies they learned in professional development. The most vivid example of this was in first grade. Three classrooms were quite similar in their literacy curriculum, in that each had guided reading groups, phonics instruction, independent reading, and centers. However, in the fourth first-grade classroom, students copied from the board, listened to basal stories, and read independently in the class library. Unfortunately, this literacy curriculum did not result in proficient readers and writers. Of all the first-grade classrooms, these children more frequently qualified for Reading Recovery support.

Spelling instruction and writing instruction were the most inconsistent across classrooms. In some classrooms, students were grouped for spelling, with two to three spelling lists. Groups were formed based on a developmental spelling inventory. In other classrooms, students used the basal text words or spelling book words, with all students expected to learn the same words. In still other classrooms, teachers created spelling lists, sometimes for the whole class and at other times for small groups. Each year, spelling was a new event for students, with no consistency in the words or strategies students were expected to learn and use.

In addition to the words, two very different strategies were presented to students for learning spelling words. The first strategy was rote memorization. In some classrooms, students were expected to memorize their spelling words for the Friday test. In other classrooms, students studied the patterns in words. They learned to apply these patterns to new words. As words became more sophisticated, they explored meaning as well. An example would be learning all long-*o* words that had an *oa* pattern in them, such as *coat*. Following this, students explored other long-*o* patterns until all these patterns were understood. Finally, they were expected to sort long-*o* words by pattern, such as *o* consonant *e*, *oa*, or *oe* (see Bear, Invernizzi, Templeton, & Johnston, 2004).

Writing instruction had similar inconsistencies. In some classrooms, students engaged in the writing process learned to draft, revise, edit, and share their work. Periodically, students wrote to fulfill their teacher's expectation, but most frequently they wrote to self-generated ideas. Writing workshop was especially prevalent in three of the third-grade classrooms. However, in many classrooms, students only used teacher-generated topics, and revision was infrequent. For example, in the fourth third-grade classroom, students wrote in journals that were passed around for student editing only, never revision. In many intermediate classrooms, students mainly wrote in preparation for the state writing assessment. Although their pieces were revised and edited, they were always written to possible assessment topics. Depending on which teacher they were assigned, students could experience few or many opportunities to engage in writing. At the end of sixth grade, there were no regular patterns in this instruction at Howard.

While I do not believe that an inconsistent vertical and horizontal alignment in literacy curriculum was evident only at Howard, I pondered what this meant for students at Howard and other elementary schools, especially schools filled with students from nonmainstream backgrounds. In some cases, students consistently benefited from rich literacy curricula throughout their elementary years. For example, with the exception of kindergarten, Eric, Fredy, Heidee, Josie, and Lucero experienced literacy curricula that included guided reading, writing process experiences, explicit instruction in phonics and spelling, book clubs, and writing to learn, as seen in math and reader response journals, throughout elementary school. Other students sporadically participated in exemplary curricula. For instance, Anthony, Bonnie, Calvin, and Maritza had narrow literacy curricula in kindergarten and first grade. Later, Anthony was enrolled in Mrs. Chew's fourth grade. So 3 of his 7 years at Howard were in less than optimal classrooms. Perhaps surprisingly, of this group, only Calvin was a struggling reader.

Certainly, having effective teachers made a difference to students at Howard (Brown, 2002). Two of these teachers are described later in this chapter. But having continuity in a literacy curriculum, paired with exemplary teaching, is equally important to students. I believe that to accelerate learning in a high-poverty school, students need a consistent rather than fragmented literacy curriculum. If, from kindergarten on, students had learned the basics of literacy, such as phonemic awareness and phonics within meaning-based reading and writing, I think more students at Howard would have reached grade-level benchmarks, no matter how they were calculated. Unfortunately, Howard students learned to value different aspects of literacy, from decoding in first grade to meaning in second. They infrequently explored informational text until second grade. Writing instruction varied from teacher to teacher. These inconsistencies made it more difficult for students to attain a rich understanding of the possibilities inherent in reading and writing.

Accelerated Reader

AR (for details about AR, see www.renlearn.com) was brought to Howard to facilitate reading achievement in 1997, at an initial cost of about $40,000. It was believed that by having a systematic, motivational reading program in place in all classrooms, students' reading achievement would be enhanced. Although teachers used this supplementary program in the primary grades, its use was more prevalent in the intermediate grades. From fourth grade on, teachers set aside daily time, at least one-half hour, for independent reading of AR books and for taking quizzes.

I found AR time to be both positive and problematic, depending on the way teachers implemented it. One positive result was that students had time each day for silent reading. They chose books based on the level determined by the STAR test. Classrooms typically had many books to choose from, and teachers supplemented these books with library books. A second positive result was that some teachers conferred with students about their reading and book selections. For instance, Mr. Bussoni encouraged students to chat about their books with him either before or after taking a quiz. Through this practice, students engaged in conversation about their books in addition to the quiz they took.

The use of AR was not all positive, however. For example in fifth grade, I often observed Maritza, as well as other students, reading simple picture books, significantly below her independent or instructional level in reading. In September she read *If You Give a Moose a Muffin* (Numeroff, 1991, level 2.9). In October she read Harry and Mudge books. Her teacher nudged her to try harder books, but Maritza persisted with these simpler texts to reach her AR goal. She discovered that quizzes were simple on these books, and she could get a perfect quiz score; thus, her goal was reached. She did not risk more difficult text, because she might not score well on the quiz, thus gaining no points to reach her goal. The result was that her teacher saw her "as substantially below level in reading. The books she chooses are not challenging. In past years, she was a higher reader, but she is struggling." Her teacher, as well as others, did not realize the strategies that students like Maritza consistently used to reach their goals. They read easy books and took easy quizzes. They did not choose chapter books or informational text, because the quizzes were seen as too difficult. The result was that independent reading time was spent reading books that were too easy for students, and not informational text or longer, more complex narratives. Thus, this practice did not enhance their reading abilities, because they stayed focused on literal comprehension of easy picture books.

A second problem with AR was that teachers and students used scores on the quizzes to determine reading achievement. This was particularly evident in Mr. McGuire's classroom. He used AR to determine reading success of students. Additionally, visible charts in the classroom documented student performance, so AR results were public to all students and visitors in the classroom. In some classrooms, students who reached their goals during a quarter had their pictures taken, and these were displayed in the room. For students who struggled with AR, these charts and photos were unpleasant daily reminders of their lack of success.

A third problem was that not all books that students wanted to read were available, because books had to have quizzes to be accessible. And although Howard had a large inventory of AR books, newer books were rarely available for reading. I only observed one teacher, Mr. Bussoni, handle this situation so that students were not limited in reading material. If a student wanted to read a book without a quiz, Mr. Bussoni asked him or her to read the book, then develop a quiz that could be added to the school's AR quizzes. Students readily took up the challenge to create quizzes for books they desired to read. Through this process, they learned about literal and inferential questions, because Mr. Bussoni decided the usual literal questions were not sufficient to document comprehension.

A fourth problem or conundrum was that while AR was in place, students' reading achievement, as measured by the norm-reference test in fourth grade, did not improve. Thus, the major goal of using

AR in the school was not achieved. The percentiles of students in the lowest quartile in reading on either the Terra Nova or ITBS assessment test follow:

- 1997–1998: 31% in the lowest quartile
- 1998–1999: 57% in the lowest quartile
- 1999–2000: 54% in the lowest quartile
- 2000–2001: 50% in the lowest quartile
- 2001–2002: 60% in the lowest quartile
- 2002–2003: 60% in the lowest quartile
- 2003–2004: 50% in the lowest quartile

Although the use of AR is not the only reason for these scores, certainly, evaluating the use of AR with respect to test scores would have been a reasonable study for the teachers and principal at Howard. However, for most teachers, the use of AR was seen as a valuable activity for students. This result in achievement test scores has been studied by others (for a synthesis of studies of AR, see readingonline.org/critical/topping/rolarL.html). In the majority of these studies, students' achievement scores have risen as a result of participation with AR, although there were issues noted in the methodology of these studies. These results are contrary to what I observed and documented in achievement test scores at Howard.

Professional Development

Schools designated as needing improvement or Title I schools were expected to select a program, such as Success for All, or a professional development program, such as CELL/ExLL, for their school. Howard chose CELL/ExLL for professional development and Reading Recovery for intervention. District personnel then studied reading achievement in these schools to see whether the program for professional development was making a difference. Overall, the results of the district study varied, and no single program was proven to be most successful. In some schools, Reading Recovery alone seemed to make a difference in third graders' achievement, with 84% of students reading at grade level in third grade in one school. In other schools, Success for All resulted in about 80% of third graders reading at grade level. Schools with CELL/ExLL also showed improvement, with about 70% of third graders reading at grade level. During this study, Howard, with both Reading Recovery and CELL/ExLL, demonstrated that about 66% of third graders read at grade level.

Howard was serious in its use of Reading Recovery and CELL/ExLL. Low-achieving first graders met with Reading Recovery teachers until they met grade-level expectations. When a new principal came to Howard, he quickly determined that Reading Recovery support was not sufficient for the needs of students at Howard. He instituted small-group support for struggling readers in second through sixth grade. Students participated in their regular literacy instruction in the classroom, then met with a reading support teacher for additional literacy instruction.

When I first observed at Howard, each Friday afternoon was set aside for professional development in literacy; later, professional development was reduced to 1 half-day each month. The literacy consultants and district consultants facilitated training in CELL/ExLL. In CELL training focused on primary students, teachers learned about supporting beginning readers through instruction of the alphabetic principle, phonemic awareness, and concepts of print in a literature-rich environment. They learned that oral language was the foundation for all literacy instruction. Specifically teachers were instructed in the following areas and/or strategies:

- Oral language
- Phonological skills
- Reading aloud
- Shared reading
- Guided reading
- Independent reading
- Interactive writing
- Independent writing

ExLL training, targeting the intermediate grades, built from this foundation and included the following:

- Phonological skills
- Reading aloud
- Shared reading
- Directed reading
- Independent reading
- Directed writing
- Independent writing
- Oral presentation

Teachers read about these strategies, discussed them at professional development sessions, and were expected to bring them into their classrooms with the support of the literacy consultants (for more details, see www.cell-exll.com). However, there was no expectation that any of these strategies must be sustained in classrooms. Guided reading groups and independent reading (AR) were the most prevalent strategies observed.

While I was observing at Howard, I noted three teachers who utilized the coaching provided by the literacy consultants. In third grade, Mrs. Erin worked with the literacy consultant in organizing routines in her classroom to include guided reading and support for writing. Mrs. Fryer, another third-grade teacher, asked the literacy consultant to model guided reading so that she could use this strategy with her lowest-level students. And Mr. McGuire worked with a literacy consultant throughout the year to develop his book club groups. Teachers were free to seek this support, and they were not required to participate in coaching sessions.

Clearly, Howard had set forth good effort to have systematic, research-based, on-site professional development with expert support. Importantly, this professional development and support were in place in 1997, long before coaching and research-based professional development were common in practice or in the literature. As seen in the earlier descriptions of teaching, many of these strategies were used in classrooms. However, there was not consistent use of these strategies at Howard. Because teachers were free to determine what strategies would be used and sustained in their classrooms, there was great variability in the way students were taught to read and write.

Another issue was that professional development took several

years to be explicitly directed to the needs of ELLs. The conversa-
tion-rich strategies recommended in CELL/ExLL were difficult to implement with ELLs. As seen in Mrs. Harter's kindergarten class, sus-
taining language-rich strategies is complicated for teachers when
students struggle with English.

I believe that Howard was forward-thinking in its implementation of professional development and support for struggling readers.
Howard personnel looked to their data, and when the needs of ELLs
became clearer, they refocused professional development to include
the needs of ELLs. Howard personnel found the necessary funds to
provide professional support for struggling readers in first grade and
beyond. They hired bilingual aides and ELL teachers to provide support for students. They implemented after-school and summer school
reading programs for struggling readers and paid teachers to lead
them. Yet, many students at Howard still struggled.

When reconsidering the professional development and support
efforts, I am led to believe that consistency was a key, an important
key, to success. If teachers had been held accountable for implementing the CELL/ExLL strategies, students would have experienced systematic, consistent instruction from kindergarten to sixth grade. Oral
language, developed in kindergarten, would have served as the foundation for other literacy instruction (Goldenberg, 2001). Students
would have consistently explored the components of literacy (phonological awareness, phonics, comprehension, vocabulary, fluency, and
writing) throughout their school careers. I believe this consistency
was necessary for the students at Howard, and certainly for other
schools with high-poverty youngsters, to develop capable readers
and writers who also scored well on achievement measures.

TWO EXEMPLARY TEACHERS

At Howard, many teachers placed student statistics first as the reason why students struggled, especially in comparison to middle-class
peers. For instance, after several teachers visited a more affluent
school, one came back and said, "All those teachers do is teach.
Their kids have no problems." Another said, "It's not possible for

our kids to perform like that. Look at their homes." Sadly, they did not view their students as able to achieve high expectations, attend college, or become leaders in their community. Mainly they saw problems when considering their students.

Unlike many of their colleagues, there were teachers at Howard who reminded me of the exceptional teachers described by Nieto (2003):

> Every day, exceptional teachers in schools throughout the nation tackle difficult circumstances in heroic but quiet ways. They do so by refusing to give in to the negative expectations that others may have of urban schools or the children who study there. (p. 52)

During my study, I was fortunate to spend time in the classrooms of extraordinary teachers—teachers who made a difference to student learning. Although there were more than two exemplary teachers at Howard, I have chosen to highlight two intermediate teachers whose teaching styles were at opposite ends of the spectrum. The first teacher puzzled me, in that she taught to the whole group and never individualized instruction for students, and her students excelled emotionally and academically. The second teacher worked constantly with individual students and quietly nudged students to reach high goals.

Mrs. Spears

On my first visit to Mrs. Spears's fourth-grade classroom, I noticed her configuration of desks—a U shape—so that she could interact and observe all of her students at one time. There were also two huge bulletin boards: One had "What Will I Be When I Grow Up?" on it, with student-constructed illustrations and text about what they planned to be; the other had "Super Stars" on it, with each student's name on a star. On the second bulletin board, students contributed words to describe themselves and their classmates, such as *awesome* and *intelligent*.

From my very first observation in August throughout the entire year, Mrs. Spears consistently complimented students publicly and privately. Often my field notes had more than 25 examples of this praise in an hour and a half of observation. For example, she said:

> "I see great work going on. I see really good artists."
> "Thank you for getting ready so quickly. Now we have time to learn."
> [to Lucero:] "I can tell that your writing is important to you. Awesome."
> "I think you are a neat class. I am learning from you."
> [when a child loses his place in class round-robin reading and another child helps:] "I love the way you helped him find his place. Now he can be a learner too."

In the final example, Mrs. Spears could have denigrated the student for losing his place; rather, she chose to reward the helping behavior.

Her focus on the positive was consistent as she managed students by providing kind rather than harsh remarks. For instance, when many students wanted to speak at the same time, she said, "Kids I love you all, but I only have two ears. I want to hear you all, so you have to raise your hands." When the behavior was more serious and such a comment was not possible, I often saw her take a student to a private part of the classroom for a serious conversation.

She was direct with her students; inappropriate behavior was not something she would tolerate. For example, Calvin often had a hard time behaving in class at the beginning of the year. One day, he loudly complained, "I hate you. You are so mean!" Mrs. Spears heard him, as did all of the students in the class. She calmly replied, "Calvin I love you for who you are. I forgive you for what you said, but I will never forget your hurtful comment." Calvin sat for a bit, but later he went over to Mrs. Spears and apologized for being "mean" to her. On another day, Calvin was in trouble for playground behavior and was called to the principal's office. Calvin mumbled about how "it wasn't fair" as he left the room. Mrs. Spears replied, "Sometimes life isn't fair, but Mrs. Spears always is." These types of comments and her consistency in expectations for behavior resulted in a classroom where students participated fully in learning activities, with no disruptions due to inappropriate behavior.

In addition to positive comments to students and consistent behavioral expectations, Mrs. Spears found ways to bring university students and other guests to her classroom. She worked with the local university to have athletes visit her room weekly to read and chat with students. When I observed these students reading, the story they chose was most often less important than the conversation they had. On one occasion, I watched as a university golfer discussed her future plans with students. She said, "I am planning on becoming a doctor. I am thinking I will be a pediatrician." After listening to her plans, students asked about her sport. Lucero asked, "Do you only play golf?" She replied that she had had to choose between basketball and golf so she could keep her grades up. This response resulted in a long discussion about grades and how to get into college. Before leaving, she offered to help students fill in paperwork to attend the local university. She said, "Your teacher will always know how to contact me. Don't forget, I want to help you."

Mrs. Spears also participated in students' out-of-school activities. She went to dance recitals, baseball games, and other events. On most of my visits, students entered her room before school, during lunch, and after school to talk with her. Students she had taught in previous years came to visit as well. Mrs. Spears also shared her personal life with students. She was planning her daughter's wedding, and students learned about several of the details. Moreover, Mrs. Spears's daughter and her husband visited school occasionally and read to students.

Whenever I asked Mrs. Spears about the focal students, she always had positive things to say. The following are some of her comments:

"Calvin is really good. He has taken up the challenge to be the best in vocabulary. He studies at home. He is learning to control his temper."

"Lucero is top-notch. She is a second teacher. She is a leader."

"Maritza is cool. She is doing great. She stays after school just to hang out with me. I love chatting with her and learning about her ambitions."

"Josie is good. She was sick last week, but she will ask others, so that she is caught up. She is totally motivated and wants to be on the Dean's list. I know she will go to college."

During our end-of-the-year interview, I asked her to reflect on her year. She said:

> "I think we had a great year. They are hard workers. They try their best—always. I love when I hear them make connections between their lives and school. I can see honesty in their writing. I love what they say about their reading. They are getting at deep meaning now, not just the surface stuff. And I am learning. I tried a lot of new things this year. I know that next year I will be better at teaching reading."

Mrs. Spears, from the very first day of fourth grade, built a classroom community that modeled respect. The students and teacher supported each other's learning, for learning was important in this classroom. Students articulated this importance at the end of the year. Josie stated, "In fourth grade I have a lot of friends and I have a good teacher. She explains things so we learn. She is nice but we have to be good students. Fifth grade is going to be easy. I think I know everything I am to learn already." Her comments demonstrate the respect that students had for Mrs. Spears, and the value and high expectations they attached to learning.

Although Mrs. Spears did not have what would be considered an exemplary literacy program (e.g., round-robin reading of the basal text followed by workbook exercises), her relationships with and expectations of students resulted in commendable learning accomplishments. Of the fourth grades, her students scored the highest on the Terra Nova, and she noted that this result "was a 15% improvement over last year." Her students also scored higher than other classes on the CRT and state writing assessments.

When her students left her classroom in June, they did so with tear-filled eyes. All hugged her good-bye, and many promised, "I will be a great student in fifth grade. I'll bring my report card by to show you."

Mr. Bussoni

Although there are many similarities between Mrs. Spears and Mr. Bussoni, such as complimenting students and being available to students throughout the day, the physical layout of their classrooms was very different. Mr. Bussoni grouped students at tables. He encouraged his students to engage in academic conversations throughout the day. And he rarely taught from the front of the room, preferring to work with small groups or individual students. Often I saw him sit next to a student and have a lengthy conversation about what the student was reading or writing. The other students in the class valued these private times and did not intrude on them. Rather, they kept reading or writing and patiently waited for their time with Mr. Bussoni.

The walls in his room were filled with student work, and there were bulletin boards focused on strategies for writing and the current topic being taught in social studies. Similar to Mrs. Spears, Mr. Bussoni had university students visit his classroom. These students worked with small groups of students using book club strategies. This reading occurred one day a week and provided additional support in reading.

After the first visit by the university students, Mr. Bussoni complimented his class. He said:

"I am proud of you. Those students walked away from here being impressed by the students at Howard. When I was at the university, there were classes and schools I never wanted to visit again. But not you. You looked them in the eye when they talked to you. They will take the letters that you wrote them about what you want to learn. They will see some mistakes because we are learning, but they will be impressed with your plans."

Following this, he clapped for them and again repeated, "I am proud of you." Comments like these indicated to students they were worthwhile individuals—individuals who had importance.

Mr. Bussoni was masterful at supporting his students as they developed reading competencies. For example, when the class was reading *Sounder* (Armstrong, 1969), he started them off with a question, "We do something every day that the boy wants to do. We take it for granted. What is it?" This question triggered a lengthy discussion. Part of this conversation follows:

STUDENT: Read.

LUCERO: He finds newspapers in the trash.

STUDENT: He reads signs in stores.

STUDENT: He finds books in trash cans.

MR. BUSSONI: Turning to page 90, I am guessing that he reads at a lower level than you do. I want you to read this part, the part that shows what he was reading.

LUCERO: I read it, but some words are hard.

MR. BUSSONI: Could you understand what it is about?

STUDENT: Cruelty.

MR. BUSSONI: That is a good connection. Why is this part hard to understand? Many adults would say it is too hard.

STUDENT: I don't understand the words like *cowardice* and *in-humane*.

MR. BUSSONI: Ninety-nine percent of kids would discard this book, but he keeps reading it. He treasures it.

STUDENT: He reads about a school he wants to go to.

STUDENT: He crosses the street because he is afraid.

MR. BUSSONI: He lives in the southern United States. There were two main groups: white and African American. So what kind of school?

STUDENT: A white school

LUCERO: African Americans couldn't go there.

STUDENT: He walks in.

MR. BUSSONI: It never says what kind of school. You figured it out. That is an inference. You did a great job figuring it out.

These conversations occurred daily both in small-group book clubs and when Mr. Bussoni read aloud. He modeled strategies such as think-aloud and guided students to deeper understanding, as seen in the preceding excerpt. His students became very aware of the strategies they used to comprehend both narrative and informational text.

Because the fifth-grade teachers worked together as a team, I interviewed them together to chat about their year. Their voices often overlapped, and the following is an amalgam of their thoughts on literacy instruction:

> "I think our literacy block was more focused this year. We had kids reading from above grade level to the first grade. So we put all the kids that were struggling or pulled out for extra support into one group, the smallest group. That meant two groups were never interrupted. It made a difference to their learning. These kids are really serious about school. School is important. They pushed themselves. They wanted to be in the highest group. And, if not in the highest group, they expected that they would exceed their goals."

Unlike previous years, these teachers knew all of the fifth graders as individuals, both emotionally and academically. All teachers were aware of the literacy strengths and needs of students, and worked to build strengths and reduce needs throughout fifth grade. This was documented in end-of-the-year outcomes as the majority of students met or exceeded grade-level expectations.

When I asked the focal students to reflect on learning to read and write throughout elementary school, most mentioned Mr. Bussoni:

> *Josie:* "In fifth grade, I learned how to read and write like really good. Mr. Bussoni made sure I read lots of books."
>
> *Lucero:* "Mr. Bussoni taught me to read and write good."
>
> *Sandra:* "Mr. Bussoni taught me to make my writing more interesting. I learned how to read more."
>
> *Maritza:* "I started to focus again on my reading. Mr. Bussoni talked to me about reading."
>
> *Maria:* "We had a lotta, lotta books. Mr. Bussoni told me that I love to read. I read to my mom and the class."
>
> *Jaryd:* "In fifth grade I started to learn about things. Mr. Bussoni helped me understand."

Mr. Bussoni expected quality work from his students, and they performed at first for him. Later, they realized the difference in who they were as readers and writers, and they challenged themselves.

FINAL LESSONS

When reflecting on such a long study of student learning and teaching, several lessons became obvious. First, teachers matter. As seen in the descriptions of Mrs. Spears and Mr. Bussoni, an exemplary teacher makes a difference to students. Maritza may have said it best in describing the effect of her teacher: "I started to focus again." Exemplary teachers can bring a student who is disengaged back to being a student participant. They can also help struggling readers become successful, and they can push successful students to newer understandings and challenges.

Second, even schools that have many of the elements associated with effective schools in place, such as a focus on improving student learning, a strong principal, strong staff collaboration, ongoing professional development, a focus on student data, and connections to parents (Taylor, Pearson, Peterson, & Rodriguez, 2005), may still not see substantial changes in student learning as measured in standardized assessments. While Howard had many elements of successful schools in place, there was no real consistency in literacy instruction from year to year. I believe that this inconsistency hampered the school's focus on improving student learning. This consistency is critical, so that students' learning in high-poverty schools can be accelerated to close the achievement gap. As one teacher observed, "One year of growth during an academic year is not enough. They regress in reading and writing over the summer. They need to grow at least a year and a half every year to reach benchmarks."

Somehow, schools need to value and support their most exemplary teachers while enhancing the literacy instruction of all teachers, so that all students can partake in rich literacy curricula. At Howard, students either participated in exemplary literacy curricula or they did not, depending on the teacher they were assigned. Looking back, this variability in instruction was problematic. Howard wanted to support teacher decision making, as seen in the freedom of implementation of strategies learned in professional development. However, this freedom meant that, in some classes, students did not write much or read for meaning. The teachers at Howard needed to find ways for every teacher to provide a consistent literacy curriculum to students, without sacrificing individual teachers' creativity and authority to make curricular decisions. This is not an easy change for teachers, but student learning, rather than teacher creativity, must be the reason behind curricular decisions.

Third, teachers at Howard and other schools with high-poverty students must put student demographics in the background. Students need not be limited academically because of the homes or neighborhoods in which they reside. Rather, teachers must know their students as more than names in an attendance book. They must find ways to know students' families, and they must encourage families to visit and participate in schools. In addition to having an academic focus, teachers must also do the following:

- Find time to talk genuinely with students.
- Be consistent, with high student and teacher expectations.
- Nurture and support students so that they are successful in attaining their goals.
- Form friendships with students and their families.
- Have confidence that their students will succeed in school and go on to be successful.

If students at Howard had participated in a school community that consistently demonstrated these values and practices, they would have felt more than safe at school: They would have known that they were respected, worthwhile individuals.

Fourth, Howard, like other elementary schools with large numbers of ELLs, needs to find ways to value parents and bring them into the school. This is no easy task. Many of Howard's teachers shared how complex it was to schedule meetings and find interpreters. Certainly, when teachers are expending considerable energy meeting the learning needs of students, this can be seen as just one more chore. However, without parent involvement, the task of increasing reading achievement at Howard is all the more difficult (Goldenberg, 2001).

Perhaps if teachers just helped to create at-home libraries for kindergartners, and had parents visit and share these books in class, children might see a closer connection between home and school. Once this foundation was established, other significant ways of partnering with parents could be developed.

Finally, this study provided a window into the complexities of learning to read and write in a high-poverty school. For students like Eric and Heidee, the road was linear; each year they became more proficient. For students like Julio, the journey was filled with detours. Sometimes, he progressed at an accelerated rate; at other times, he seemed to regress to previous strategies and understandings. For students like Anthony and Calvin, the personal connection with a teacher determined their learning journey. These varied paths to reading and writing proficiency demonstrate the following:

- The importance of trust and respect between teachers and students for student learning.
- The importance of effective teachers, who have high expectations for students, as critical to student learning.
- The importance of caring teachers who support student learning.
- The importance of the belief that students, no matter what their home circumstances, can successfully learn.

REFERENCES

Armstrong, W. (1969). *Sounder.* New York: HarperCollins.

Bear, D., Invernizzi, M., Templeton, S., & Johnston, F. (2004). *Words their way: Word study for phonics, vocabulary, and spelling instruction* (3rd ed.). Upper Saddle River, NJ: Prentice-Hall.

Brown, D. (2002). *Becoming a successful urban teacher.* Portsmouth, NH: Heinemann.

Calkins, L., Montgomery, K., Santman, D., & Falk, B. (1998). *A teacher's guide to standardized reading tests: Knowledge is power.* Portsmouth, NH: Heinemann.

Dillon, D. (2000). *Reconsidering how to meet the literacy needs of all students.* Newark, DE: International Reading Association.

Goldenberg, C. (2001). Making schools work for low-income families in the

21st century. In S. B. Neuman & D. K. Dickinson (Eds.), *Handbook of early literacy research* (Vol. 1, pp. 211–231). New York: Guilford Press.

Hoffman, J., Assaf, L., & Paris, S. (2001). High-stakes testing in reading: Today in Texas, tomorrow? *Reading Teacher, 54*, 482–494.

Nieto, S. (2003). *What keeps teachers going?* New York: Teachers College Press.

Numeroff, L. (1991). *If you give a moose a muffin.* New York: HarperCollins.

Smith, M. (1991). Put to the test: The effects of external testing on teachers. *Educational Researcher, 20*, 8–11.

Taylor, B., Pearson, P. D., Peterson, D., & Rodriguez, M. (2005). The CIERA school change framework: An evidence-based approach to professional development and school reading improvement. *Reading Research Quarterly, 40*, 40–69.

Appendix

Methodology of
the Research Study

For readers interested in a more detailed explanation of the method used to guide this study, I have provided a full description of the method in this Appendix.

DESIGN

I chose a longitudinal multicase study design for this research project (Yin, 1994). By utilizing this design, I was able to explore literacy learning and instruction without overtly manipulating the classroom context (Merriam, 1998). Moreover, case study research is most appropriate when the researcher has "little control over events, and when the focus is on a contemporary phenomenon within some real-life context" (Yin, 1994, p. 1). The case studies of the teachers and students are descriptive and provide an overview of instruction and learning from kindergarten to sixth grade.

RESEARCHER STANCE

I entered this study with experience in longitudinal case study research (Barone, 1999). I had followed a group of students from preschool through the primary grades to describe them as literacy learners. I have been a teacher of first graders, second graders, and third graders in high-poverty schools and have brought these personal experiences to this study (Connelly & Clandinin, 1999). In most of this teaching, I worked with children considered to be at risk because of their home demographics.

I also have strong beliefs grounded in research that document how children and teachers construct knowledge together (DeVries & Kohlberg, 1987; Vygotsky, 1978). I believe that literacy is a social enterprise grounded in communication (Rodriquez, 1999). Although I believe that the teacher is critical to the learning of students, not a specific program, I also know that certain literacy practices are more beneficial than others for readers and writers (Pressley, Rankin, & Yokoi, 1996). I also believe that children who attend high-poverty schools can become readers and writers who can both decode text and understand its meanings. I value teachers in such settings who have high expectations for students and help them achieve them (Padron, Waxman, Brown, & Powers, 2000).

SETTING

Howard Elementary School (pseudonyms are used) was chosen as the site for this study (see Table A.1. for a 2003–2004 summary report and overview of the demographics of Howard). It is one of the older schools in a midsize school district in a western U.S. city. The neighborhood surrounding the school is eclectic in that it consists of single- and multiple-family homes, apartments, and public housing. This school has always been known for its high enrollment of minority students and its low standardized test scores. It has consistently been on the state's *needs improvement* list and had a state team assigned to it to help with achievement.

Because of low standardized test scores, the school focused on literacy instruction as a way to raise scores. In the primary grades, mornings were set aside for literacy instruction, balanced to include the following elements: oral language, phonological skills, read-aloud, shared reading, guided reading, independent reading, interactive writing, and independent writing. In the intermediate grades, afternoons were set aside for literacy instruction. Students were expected to read, write, and learn to spell. To help teachers, professional development, most often focused on literacy, was provided each Friday afternoon; later, this was changed to once per month. Additionally, there were two reading consultants in the school, and Reading Recovery was available for qualifying first graders.

**TABLE A.1. Summary Report and Overview of Demographics
of Howard Elementary School**

Summary report

Celebrations

1. Implemented a year-round schedule to address needs of students.
2. Made AYP in 2002–2003.
3. Four teachers became National Board Certified Teachers.
4. Many teachers participated in profession development targeted to needs of ELL students.
5. 2003–2004 writing scores increased for fourth and sixth graders.
6. Read 180 was implemented as a reading tutorial for fourth, fifth, and sixth graders.

Goals

1. Increase achievement in reading comprehension.
2. Put more emphasis on vocabulary instruction to improve student understanding.
3. Continue to focus on writing instruction.

	Demographics						
	Enrollment no.		Enrollment %		Avg. daily attendance		
	School	District	School	District	School	District	State
Total students	608	60,125			95.1	95.3	94.1
Male	289	30,897	47.5	51.4			
Female	319	29,228	52.5	48.6			
American Indian/Alaskan Native	14	1,676	2.3	2.8	95.2	93.7	92.3
Asian/Pacific Islander	67	3,641	11.0	6.1	94.0	95.4	95.7
Hispanic	411	16,229	67.6	27.0	95.4	95.2	94.0
Black/African American	53	2,137	8.7	3.6	95.4	94.7	93.0
White	63	36,442	10.4	60.6	93.5	95.4	94.2
IEP	54	7,572	8.9	12.6	94.8	94.1	92.5
LEP	286	8,126	47.0	13.5	95.2	95.7	94.7
FRL	530	18,741	87.2	31.2	95.3	95.2	94.1

Note. IEP, students with disabilities; LEP, students with limited English proficiency; FRL, students qualifying for free/reduced lunch.

PARTICIPANTS

Children

I identified 16 focal children during their first week of kindergarten. During this week, the teachers met with each child individually for testing purposes. I met with parents while their child was assessed to gain their permission for their child to be included in the study. A bilingual aide helped me with this process.

I selected a focal group of children, balanced in gender and representative of the ethnic diversity within the school. Nine children were of Hispanic origin (country of origin was Mexico except for one child from El Salvador), one child was from the Philippines, two children were African American, and three children were European Americans. (One student moved two weeks into the study and is not discussed.) Ten of the focal children were learning English as a new language. Only four of these children had any preschool experiences.

Teachers

I followed students to the classroom to which they were assigned. Table A.2 documents the experience of the teachers and their typical classroom instruction.

DATA COLLECTION

Throughout the study, I observed the students, interviewed their teachers and principal, and collected work samples. I had a doctoral student, experienced in taking field notes, simultaneously observe in each classroom to ensure reliability in the observational notes and to guard against any bias on my part. She also debriefed me on the tentative findings and helped to construct a synthesis of the findings. More specific descriptions of the data collection process follows.

Observation

The children were observed on a weekly basis. On most days, I observed during the time set aside for literacy instruction. In the primary grades, the morning was set aside for literacy instruction; in the intermediate grades, the afternoon. There were no intercom messages or special classes during this time. At the beginning and end of each school year, I observed a whole day of instruction. In this way, I could see how literacy instruction was imbed-

TABLE A.2. Teacher Experience and Typical Classroom Instruction

Grade level	Teachers and classroom instruction			
Kindergarten	Mrs. Harter	Mrs. Martin & Mrs. George		
	(15 years) Read-aloud Take-home books Phonics activities Alphabet journals Personal words worksheets	(Martin—11 years; George—3 years) Read-aloud Take-home books Alphabet journals Phonics worksheets		
First grade	Mrs. Kirby & Ms. Mears	Mrs. Cullen & Mrs. Adams	Mr. Shott & Mrs. Sims	Mrs. Messina & Mrs. Denton
	(Kirby—4 years; Mears—2 years) Word wall Independent reading Reading groups Centers Phonics instruction Journals Shared reading Guided reading Interactive writing Reading buddies	(Cullen—5 years; Adams—6 years) Word wall Independent reading Reading groups Phonics instruction Story time	(Shott—7 years; Sims—7 years) Word wall Independent reading Reading groups Centers Phonics instruction Journals Shared reading Guided reading Spelling tests	(Messina—15 years; Denton—7 years) Word wall Independent reading Reading groups Centers Phonics instruction Journals Guided reading Spelling tests Computers
Second grade	Mrs. Scott & Mrs. Ford	Mrs. Stewart & Mrs. Harrison	Mrs. Stevens & Mrs. Smith	
	(Scott—1 year; Ford—5 years) DOL Spelling lists grouped by ability Narrative and informational text Writing Journals Reading groups Basal text Read-aloud for writing Think, pair, share	(Stewart—First year; Harrison—20 years) DOL Spelling lists grouped by ability Narrative and informational text Writing Journals Reading groups Basal text Word study Author's chair	(Stevens—2 years; Smith—2 years) DOL Spelling lists grouped by ability Narrative and informational text Writing Journals Reading groups Basal text Oral language vocabulary	

(continued)

TABLE A.2. (*continued*)

Grade level	Teachers and classroom instruction			
Third grade	Mrs. Fryer	Mrs. Walker	Mrs. Erin	Ms. Read
	(First year)	(6 years)	(4 years)	(7 years)
	Circle–seat–center organization	Word study	Writing workshop	Journals
	Reading groups (3–4)	DOL	Read-aloud	Read-aloud
	DOL	AR	Word wall	DOL
	Workbook	Read-alouds	DOL	Reading groups
	Read-aloud	Word wall	Spelling books	Reading buddies
	Word wall	Writing workshop	Reading groups (4)	Word wall
	Writing workshop	Centers	Assessment— Informal Reading Inventory	Assessment— running records
	Journals	Reading groups (5)		
		Comprehension instruction		
		Assessment— reading records		
Fourth grade	Mrs. Chew	Mrs. Spears	Mrs. Scott	
	(2 years)	(4 years)	(2 years)	
	Whole-class literature series	Whole-class literature series	DOL	
	DOL	DOL	Read-aloud	
	Whole-class vocabulary	Sustained Silent Reading	Whole-class literature series	
	Spelling list	4 reading groups	Reading buddies	
	AR	Word sorts	Word jar	
	Homework—read 20 min.	Homework—read 20 min.	Reading groups (kids read orally)	
	Reading buddies	Spelling list	Packets of worksheets	
	Book club groups (oral reading)			
	Worksheets at stations			
Fifth grade	Mrs. Callep	Mr. Bussoni	Mrs. Katen	
	(6 years)	(17 years)	(2 years)	
	Students grouped by ability. Each teacher takes a group.			
	Spelling (word study)			
	Journals			
	AR			
	Book club			
	Writing			

TABLE A.2. (*continued*)

Sixth grade	Ms. Booth	Mr. McGuire & Ms. Jones
	(20 years)	(McGuire—2 years; Jones—14 years)
	Reading groups/ book club	McGuire took both classes for literacy
		Word study in groups—varied lists
	Writing	Book club
	Vocabulary	AR
	Reading aloud to class	Journals
	Reading and writing in content areas	Writing
	Spelling from textbook	

Note. AR, Accelerated reader; DOL, daily oral language.

ded in other content-based instruction. For each child, I created a literacy profile based on these observations. These profiles, as well as all field notes, were shared with the teachers for accuracy checks. The teachers often contributed additional information that helped me to understand the literacy development of individual children.

Interviews

The teachers were formally interviewed at least twice per year. At the beginning of the year, I asked them about their goals and how they viewed each of the focal children as literacy learners. At the end of year, interviews focused on the whole year and what they thought went well and what issues had proved problematic in their literacy instruction and the learning of their students. I also had informal chats with the teachers during each of my visits to their classrooms. I tape recorded and transcribed end-of-the-year interviews.

Artifacts

I collected work samples from the students. I also entered in my computer samples of their reading and the conversations they had with their teachers. I collected informal assessments conducted by the teachers.

DATA ANALYSIS

The data were analyzed with an interpretive approach. I sought to understand the teaching and learning in these classrooms (Erickson, 1986). To accomplish this goal, I reviewed all data routinely and built individual profiles of each child's learning. I also compiled descriptions of the typical teaching provided to the students. I noted teachers' practices, groupings, and expectations for their students.

Throughout data collection, I made cross-case comparisons among the children to note differences and similarities in development. I also noted whether there were any teacher effects in their development, for example, whether all the children in one class had accelerated or delayed development. I used the rich pictures of literacy instruction in each classroom as the backdrop for a better understanding of each child's literacy development. So, for instance, if teachers only focused on lower-level skills, then it would be difficult for children to discover the meaning-making aspects of reading and writing. Simply saying that a child had not developed these literacy understandings would not reflect the synergy between teaching and learning.

REFERENCES

Barone, D. (1999). *Resilient children: Stories of poverty, drug exposure, and literacy development.* Newark, DE: International Reading Association.

Connelly, F., & Clandinin, D. (Eds.). (1999). *Shaping a professional identity.* New York: Teachers College Press.

DeVries, R., & Kohlberg, L. (1987). *Programs of early education: The constructivist view.* White Plains, NY: Longman.

Erickson, F. (1986). Qualitative methods in research on teaching. In M. Wittrock (Ed.), *Handbook of research on teaching* (3rd ed., pp. 119–161). Washington, DC: American Educational Research Association.

Merriam, S.B. (1998). *The case study research in education.* San Francisco: Jossey-Bass.

Padron, Y., Waxman, H., Brown, A., & Powers, R. (2000). *Improving classroom instruction and student learning for resilient and non-resilient English language learners.* Santa Cruz, CA: Center for Research on Education, Diversity, and Excellence.

Pressley, M., Rankin, J., & Yokoi, L. (1996). A survey of instructional practices of primary grade teachers nominated as effective in promoting literacy. *Elementary School Journal, 96,* 363–384.

Rodriquez, M. (1999). Literacy experiences of three young Dominican children in New York City: Implications for teaching in urban settings. *Educators for Urban Minorities, 1,* 19–31.

Vygotsky, L. (1978). *Thought and language.* Cambridge, MA: MIT Press.

Yin, R. (1994). *Case study research: Design and methods* (3rd ed.). Thousand Oaks, CA: Sage.

Index

"f" following a page number indicates a figure; "t" following a page number indicates a table.

A Girl from Yamhill (Cleary), 1–2
Accelerated Reader (AR), 163–165
Achievement, grade-level. *see also under individual grades*
  Accelerated Reader (AR) and, 164–165
  collaborative learning and, 117
  conundrums regarding, 157–160
  in second grade, 46t
  in third grade, 51
  in fifth grade, 62
  in sixth grade, 67–68
  Reading Recovery and CELL/ExLL implementation, 166
  summary of, 26t–32t
  variations in, 71–72
Alphabetic principle
  grade-level achievement and, 72
  understanding and using, 6
Assessments, grade-level achievement and, 157–159. *see also* High-stakes testing

C

Classroom climate
  high-stakes testing and, 154–155
  positioning theory and, 137
  social constructivism model and, 116–117
  students from high-poverty backgrounds and, 8
  teachers and, 12
Collaborative learning
  literacy development and, 148
  positioning theory and, 131–132
  social constructivism model and, 116–126
Communication between home and school
  English language learners and, 155–157
  teachers and, 177–178
Comprehension
  comparisons of instructional practices and, 101–103
  instruction in, 9
  in the intermediate grades, 7
  struggling readers and ELLs, 74–75
  teachers in the research study and, 92
Comprehensive Early Literacy Learning/Extended Literacy Learning (CELL/ExLL). *see also* Professional development
  conundrums regarding, 165–168
  overview, 80, 152
Curriculum, consistency of, 160–163, 176–177

D

Daily oral language (DOL) activities
    comparisons of instructional
        practices and, 107
    in second grade, 47–48
    in fourth grade, 58
    teachers in the research study and,
        93
Decoding skills
    in first grade, 41, 90
    grade-level achievement and, 72
    teachers in the research study and,
        91
Developmental processes
    nonlinear view of, 115
    overview, 147–148
    positioning theory of, 116, 126–
        141
    resilience theory and, 116, 141–
        147
    social constructivism model of,
        115, 116–126

E

Engagement
    collaborative learning and, 117
    positioning theory and, 126–141
English language learners
    comparisons of instructional
        practices and, 109–111
    instruction and, 14–16
    oral language and, 37–39
    Reading Recovery and, 41–42
    relationships between schools and
        parents and, 155–157
    resilience theory and, 144
    support for, 74–75
    teachers in the research study and,
        87–88
Environment, classroom/school
    high-stakes testing and, 154–155
    positioning theory and, 137
    social constructivism model and,
        116–117
    students from high-poverty
        backgrounds and, 8
    teachers and, 12

Expectations of students
    assessments and, 157–159
    conforming to, 72–73
    English language learners, 14
    students from high-poverty
        backgrounds and, 8

F

Field trips, 91–92
Fifth grade
    exemplary example of, 172–176
    literacy instruction during, 61–66
    positioning theory and, 136–139
    resilience theory and, 146–147
    teachers in the research study and,
        13, 83t, 85, 95–98
First grade
    expectations for reading and
        writing during, 5
    literacy instruction during, 40–44,
        43f
    positioning theory and, 129–131
    social constructivism model and,
        118–121
    teachers in the research study and,
        10, 81t, 85, 89–92
Fluency
    instruction in, 9, 105–106
    in the intermediate grades, 7
Fourth grade
    exemplary example of, 168–172
    informational text during, 7
    literacy instruction during, 55–61
    positioning theory and, 134–136
    resilience theory and, 144–146
    teachers in the research study and,
        13, 83t, 85, 92–95
Friendships
    expectations of students and, 73
    in sixth grade, 66

G

Grade-level achievement. *see also*
        under individual grades
    Accelerated Reader (AR) and, 164–
        165
    collaborative learning and, 117

conundrums regarding, 157–160
in second grade, 46t
in third grade, 51
in fifth grade, 62
in sixth grade, 67–68
Reading Recovery and CELL/
ExLL implementation, 166
summary of, 26t–32t
variations in, 71–72
Graphic organizers, 92
Group work, 91. see also
Collaborative learning

H

High-stakes testing
Accelerated Reader (AR) and, 164–
165
collaborative learning and, 116–
126
conundrums regarding, 152–155,
153t, 154t
in third grade, 51
in fourth grade, 57–58
in fifth grade, 62–63
teachers in the research study and,
95

I

Independent reading time
in fourth grade, 55
in fifth grade, 61–62
in sixth grade, 67
teachers and, 11
Instruction. see also Literacy learning
and instruction; Teachers
comparisons of, 98–111
conundrums regarding, 151–168,
153t, 154t, 176–177
English language learners and, 14–
16
exemplary examples of, 168–176
in the research study, 5–8
for students from high-poverty
backgrounds, 8–13
Instruction, phonics
comparisons of instructional
practices and, 99–101

importance of, 9
during kindergarten, 35
Instruction, spelling
consistency of, 161
teachers in the research study and,
93–94, 96
Instructional aides, use of, 74
Intermediate grades. see also Fifth
grade; Fourth grade; Sixth
grade
assessments and, 158
expectations for reading and
writing during, 6–8
literacy instruction during, 11–13
teachers in the research study and,
92–98
Invented spelling, 6

K

Kindergarten
literacy learning during, 33–40, 36f
positioning theory and, 128–129
teachers in the research study and,
10, 81t, 85, 86–89

L

Language development, 14–15
Learning literacy. see Literacy
learning and instruction
Letter knowledge
grade-level achievement and, 72
importance of, 6
during kindergarten, 35–37, 36f
Literacy development
nonlinear view of, 115
overview, 147–148
positioning theory of, 116, 126–
141
resilience theory and, 116, 141–
147
social constructivism model of,
115, 116–126
Literacy learning and instruction
conforming to expectations and,
72–73
conundrums regarding, 151–168,
153t, 154t

Literacy learning and instruction
     (*continued*)
  in kindergarten, 33–40, 36*f*
  in first grade, 40–44, 43*f*
  in second grade, 45–49, 46*t*
  in third grade, 49–55
  in fourth grade, 55–61
  in fifth grade, 61–66
  in sixth grade, 66–70
  grade-level achievement and, 71–72
  overview of end-of-year results,
     26*t*–32*t*
  in the research study, 5–8
  social constructivism model and,
     116–126
  struggling readers and ELLs, 74–
     75
  teachers in the research study and,
     86–92
Longitudinal studies, 2–4. *see also*
     Research study methodology

M

Making Words strategy, 53–54
Matthew effect, 2–3
Methodology of the research study
  data analysis, 187–188
  data collection, 184, 187
  design, 181
  participants, 184, 185*t*–187*t*
  setting, 182, 183*t*
  stance of researcher, 181–182
Motivation of the student, 6
Multisyllabic words, 7–8

N

Name writing, during kindergarten,
     35–37, 36*f*
National Board certification
     activities, 80. *see also*
     Professional development
National Reading Panel report
     (2000), 9
No Child Left Behind, 160
Note writing during class
  expectations of students and, 73
  in sixth grade, 66

O

Oral language. *see also* Daily oral
     language (DOL) activities
  during kindergarten, 37–39
  teachers in the research study and,
     92

P

Parent–school relationship
  English language learners and,
     155–157
  resilience theory and, 142–147
  students from high-poverty
     backgrounds and, 8
  teachers and, 177–178
Parental involvement
  English language learners and,
     155–157
  teachers and, 177–178
Peer relationships
  expectations of students and,
     73
  in sixth grade, 66
Phonemic awareness
  comparisons of instructional
     practices and, 98–99
  grade-level achievement and, 72
  teachers in the research study and,
     90
Phonics instruction
  comparisons of instructional
     practices and, 99–101
  importance of, 9
  during kindergarten, 35
Phonics skills
  during first grade, 44
  grade-level achievement and, 72
  teachers in the research study and,
     90
Phonological awareness
  importance of, 6
  instruction in, 9
Positioning theory, 116, 126–141
Poverty
  instruction and, 8–13
  resilience theory and, 141
  teachers and, 177–178

Primary grades. *see also* First grade;
    Kindergarten; Second grade;
    Third grade
  achievement during, 5–6
  assessments and, 158
  literacy instruction during, 9–11
  teachers in the research study and,
    86–92
Print functions, 6
Professional development
  Comprehensive Early Literacy
    Learning/Extended Literacy
    Learning (CELL/ExLL), 152
  conundrums regarding, 165–168
  in the research study, 18, 79–
    80
  teachers in the research study and,
    88

R

Read-alouds, 118–121
Reading. *see also* Literacy learning
    and instruction
  in kindergarten, 39
  in first grade, 41–42
  in second grade, 45–47
  in third grade, 50–52
  in fourth grade, 56–58
  in fifth grade, 61–63
  in sixth grade, 66–68
Reading comprehension
  comparisons of instructional
    practices and, 101–103
  instruction in, 9
  in the intermediate grades, 7
  struggling readers and ELLs, 74–
    75
  teachers in the research study and,
    92
Reading Recovery
  compared to professional
    development, 165–166
  consistency of curriculum and, 161
  during first grade, 41–42
  grade-level achievement and, 71
  struggling readers and ELLs, 75
  teachers in the research study and,
    91

Relationship between teacher and
    students
  resilience theory and, 142–147
  students from high-poverty
    backgrounds and, 8
Relationship, parent–school
  English language learners and,
    155–157
  teachers and, 177–178
Relationships, peer
  expectations of students and, 73
  in sixth grade, 66
Research study. *see also* Research
    study methodology; *under
    individual grades*
  comparisons of instructional
    practices and, 98–111
  overview of, 16–20, 19*t*
  students in, 26*t*–32*t*
  teachers in, 80, 81*t*–84*t*, 85–86,
    111–112
Research study methodology
  data analysis, 187–188
  data collection, 184, 187
  design, 181
  participants, 184, 185*t*–187*t*
  setting, 182, 183*t*
  stance of researcher, 181–182
Resilience theory, 116, 141–147
Resistance of the student, 126–141
Retelling of a story, 39
Routines, classroom, 12

S

School–parent relationship
  English language learners and,
    155–157
  teachers and, 177–178
Schools, effective, 176
Science, teaching through reading, 91
Second grade
  literacy instruction during, 45–49,
    46*t*
  positioning theory and, 131–132
  resilience theory and, 143–144
  teachers in the research study and,
    10, 82*t*, 85, 89–92
Self-identification of students, 5

Sixth grade
  literacy instruction during, 66–70
  positioning theory and, 139–140
  social constructivism model and,
      123–126
  teachers in the research study and,
      84t, 85, 95–98
Social constructivism, 115, 116–126
Social studies, teaching through
      reading, 91
Sound–symbol knowledge
  grade-level achievement and, 72
  during kindergarten, 35–37, 36f
  teachers in the research study and,
      91
Spelling instruction
  consistency of, 161
  teachers in the research study and,
      93–94, 96
Spelling skills
  in second grade, 48–49
  in fourth grade, 60
Standardized testing
  Accelerated Reader (AR) and, 164–
      165
  collaborative learning and, 116–
      126
  conundrums regarding, 152–155,
      153t, 154t
  in third grade, 51
  in fourth grade, 57–58
  in fifth grade, 62–63
  teachers in the research study and,
      95
Struggling readers. see also Grade-
      level achievement
  over time, 2–4
  support for, 74–75
Students, expectations of
  assessments and, 157–159
  conforming to, 72–73
  English language learners, 14
  students from high-poverty
      backgrounds and, 8
Students in the research study, 18–
      19, 184
Success for All program, 166
Sustained reading and writing, 7

Sustained Silent Reading
  in fourth grade, 55
  in fifth grade, 61–62

T

Teachers
  comparisons of instructional
      practices, 98–111
  consistency of instruction and,
      162–163, 176–177
  exemplary examples of, 168–176
  importance of, 8–9, 79–80, 176
  in intermediate grades, 12–13, 92–
      98
  in primary grades, 10–11, 86–92
  professional development and, 18,
      79–80, 88, 152, 165–168
  qualities possessed by, 10–11, 13
  in the research study, 18, 80, 81t–
      84t, 85–86, 86–98, 111–112,
      185t–187t
  resilience theory and, 142
Testing, standardized
  Accelerated Reader (AR) and, 164–
      165
  collaborative learning and, 116–
      126
  conundrums regarding, 152–155,
      153t, 154t
  in third grade, 51
  in fourth grade, 57–58
  in fifth grade, 62–63
  teachers in the research study and, 95
Third grade
  literacy instruction during, 49–55
  positioning theory and, 132–134
  social constructivism model and,
      121–123
  teachers in the research study and,
      10, 82t, 85, 89–92
Token economy, 95–96
Turnaround teachers, 142–143

V

Vocabulary
  importance of, 6
  instruction in, 9, 103–105

in the intermediate grades, 7
in third grade, 51–52
in sixth grade, 70
struggling readers and ELLs, 74–
75
teachers in the research study and,
92–93

W

Word study
in first grade, 44
in second grade, 48–49
in third grade, 53–54
in fourth grade, 60
in fifth grade, 64–65
in sixth grade, 69–70

Writing skills
during first grade, 42–44,
43f
in second grade, 47–48
in third grade, 52–53
in fourth grade, 58–60
in fifth grade, 63–64
in sixth grade, 68–69
high-stakes testing and, 153–154,
153t, 154t
instruction in, 107–109, 161–
162
social constructivism model and,
121–123
teachers in the research study and,
91, 94–95, 96